CIGARS

NICHOLAS FOULKES

9 10 8

Preface Publishing
20 Vauxhall Bridge Road
London SW1V 2SA

Preface Publishing is part of the Penguin Random House group of companies whose
addresses can be found at global.penguinrandomhouse.com.

Penguin
Random House
UK

First published by Preface Publishing in 2017

www.penguin.co.uk

A CIP catalogue record for this book is available from the British Library.

ISBN 9781848094871

Designed by Tim Barnes ⌇ herechickychicky.com

Printed and bound by C&C Offset Printing Co., Ltd.

CONTENTS

INTRODUCTION

A good cigar is more than one of life's consolations; it is the promise of a piece of heaven on earth. Too far-fetched? Certainly Mark Twain did not think so. A man who could never resist a truth wrapped in a witty apothegm, Twain once said, 'If smoking is not allowed in heaven I shall not go.'

It was my wife's stepfather who introduced me to what he identifies as 'the feeling of well-being' that accompanies a cigar. A cigar is about more than mere tobacco. There are many more effective and less expensive ways of delivering nicotine into the bloodstream. What the cigar offers is a window onto an entire world and insight into a fascinating culture, a culture that in some ways has changed little in centuries.

I certainly never imagined that the Montecristo No. 4 that my stepfather-in-law handed me over twenty-five years ago would take me on a journey, involving many visits to Cuba and the Dominican Republic, to the coveted Havana Man of the Year Award, but above all to what has become an abiding interest in the history, traditions, techniques, characters, tobacco and lands involved in creating the cultural object that is the cigar. I have written this book not so much as an expert, but rather as an amateur in the old sense, trying to convey my enthusiasm for the cigar and its remarkable world. Since my first visit to Cuba over twenty years ago, I have written the 'Bolívar' column in *Country Life*, a sporadically appearing collection of jottings on what I have encountered along this fascinating and unfinished journey and I have also contributed to the *Financial Times' How to Spend It*. Some of what follows is gleaned from those pages.

This book is part almanac, part guide, part personal account, and I hope it contains some information that is of use, or at least of mild interest, whether you have yet to fall under the spell of the cigar or whether you are already a seasoned collector.

And talking of magic and spells: 'It all started in the New World,' wrote G. Cabrera Infante, 'where smoking was not for gentlemen but for sorcerers – and for the incumbent Indian chief: he who wore the feathers.'[1] The inhabitants of the 'New World' discovered by Columbus consumed tobacco for, amongst other things, spiritual refreshment and enlightenment. The shaman entered a trance, in which state he would be imparted with whatever divine wisdom was available.

[1]   G. Cabrera Infante, *Holy Smoke*, p.2

Of course, tobacco was one of the mysterious plants brought back to Europe by those first explorers of the lands across the ocean, and so commenced what Infante describes as 'the five-century-old relationship between the European gentleman and his smoke'.[2]

It is hard to identify what it is that accounts for the appeal of the cigar. Certainly its enthusiasts over the centuries have credited it with miraculous powers. For Victor Hugo, 'tobacco is the plant that converts thoughts into dreams'. P.J. O'Rourke, meanwhile, claimed in an interview with *Cigar Aficionado* magazine: 'I really think cigar smoking does make you smarter. Or maybe it just makes you sit still long enough to be smart.' As far as Thackeray was concerned, a cigar was an emotional Swiss Army knife: 'The cigar has been one of the greatest creature comforts of my life, a kind companion – a great stimulant – a cementer of friendships.' While for Evelyn Waugh it was a perfect panacea, gently caressing and restorative: 'the most futile and disastrous day seems well spent when it is reviewed through the blue fragrant smoke of a Havana cigar'.[3] And while it may not have provided European gentlemen with the hotline to the gods that the native inhabitants of the Americas enjoyed, Waugh's 'blue fragrant smoke' has proved adept at summoning inspiration. Calliope, the muse of epic poetry, was certainly in the room (smoke-filled, one hopes) with Lord Byron in 1823, when the mad, bad and dangerous-to-know poet was composing *The Island*, one of his multi-canto extravaganzas. At times I find

---

[2] Ibid.

[3] Quoted in promotional brochure *Havanas, a Unique Blend of Sun, Soil, and Skill* (Hunters & Frankau Ltd., South Africa, 1994).

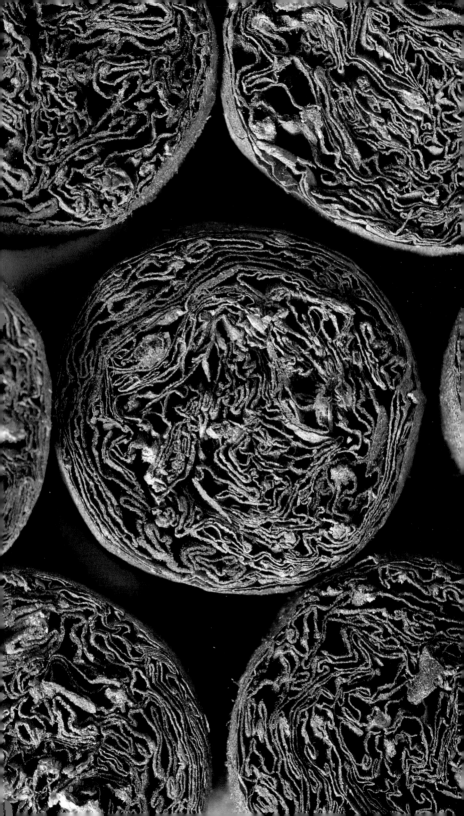

Byron a little too rich for my taste, and I lack the breadth of knowledge of classical literature to get the most out of it without having to refer to endless footnotes, but the professional rebel's affection for a good cigar is clear even to me.

> *Sublime Tobacco, which from east to west*
> *Cheers the tar's labour or the Turkman's rest;*
> *Which on the Moslem's ottoman divides*
> *His hours, and rivals opium and his brides:*
> *Magnificent in Stamboul, but less grand,*
> *Tho not less loved in Wapping and the Strand:*
> *Divine in hookahs, glorious in a pipe,*
> *When tipp'd with amber, mellow, rich, and ripe:*
> *Like other charmers, wooing the caress*
> *More dazzlingly when daring in full dress:*
> *Yet thy true lovers more admire by far*
> *The naked beauties – Give me a Cigar.*

Rudyard Kipling went even further and articulated the views of many men of his age when he wrote what by today's standards is the misogynistic maxim: 'a woman is only a woman, but a good Cigar is a Smoke'. This observation comes in the penultimate couplet of 'The Betrothed' (subtitle: '"You must choose between me and your cigar" – Breach of Promise Case, circa 1885'), in which the narrator is forced to choose between his fiancée and his cigars:

> *Open the old cigar-box,*
> *get me a Cuba stout,*
> *For things are running crossways,*
> *and Maggie and I are out.*

We quarrelled about Havanas –
we fought o'er a good cheroot,
And I knew she is exacting,
and she says I am a brute.

After numerous couplets weighing the relative merits of cigar smoking and marriage, he comes to his conclusion

Open the old cigar-box –
let me consider anew –
Old friends, and who is Maggie
that I should abandon you?
A million surplus Maggies
are willing to bear the yoke;
And a woman is only a woman,
but a good Cigar is a Smoke.
Light me another Cuba –
I hold to my first-sworn vows.
If Maggie will have no rival,
I'll have no Maggie for Spouse!

It is a pity that this poem has been overshadowed by its downright sexist message, as it has another message too, not least about the beauty, charm and seductive power of 'that harem of dusky beauties, fifty tied in a string' (again I am sure that a critical early-twenty-first-century reader of this late-nineteenth-century line would find much to decry). It tells of the infinite variety of the world of the cigar, how each smouldering finger of tobacco, in transforming itself into fine powdery ash and fragrant smoke, transports the person enjoying it to another part of the world: the romantic

Spanish Main and of course sultry Havana, at the time Kipling was writing still the pearl of Spain's Latin American empire.

I am more uxorious than the narrator of this poem, but I can also identify with his feelings for the cigar. Much may have changed since the late nineteenth century, not least attitudes towards gender and smoking, but the lure of the cigar's harem, its siren song, is as compelling as ever. To call it a vice or an addiction is to demean the centuries of tradition and the work of the growers, blenders and rollers: this is not so much smoking as taking pleasure in life, slowing down to enjoy the way a cigar looks, its gentle aroma and its complex and lingering flavours. Each cigar enjoyed is a small victory, a gift from life, a moment crystallised, time rescued from the ceaseless momentum of the modern world. Above all it is an instrument of pleasure, a fact that no one has articulated more accurately than Prince Stepan Arkadyich Oblonsky, the good-humoured man of the world in Anna Karenina: 'A cigar – it's not so much a pleasure as the crown and hallmark of pleasure.'[4]

---

[4]   Leo Tolstoy, *Anna Karenina*, p.162

HISTORY

The Indies. In the fifteenth century, these three syllables evoked a world beyond the imaginings of most Europeans. India, China, Japan, Arabia, the steppes of Asia Minor, the realm of Prester John, the legendary Christian king and descendant of one of the three Magi, monsters, gold mines, spices, silks ... all this and more fell under the heading of the Indies.

It was a place of perils but also of immense riches, and by the end of the century, a Genoese mariner called Cristóbal Colón [*above*] – also known as Christopher Columbus – had become obsessed with the idea of finding a western sea route there. Flushed with the recent routing of the Saracens from Andalusia, King Ferdinand and Queen Isabella were prepared to back him in his quest. And so on 3 August 1492, Colón set off with a crew of 87 and a flotilla of three ships: the 100-ton *Santa Maria*, the 60-ton *Pinta* and the 50-ton *Nina*. He had instructions to contact the local king on his arrival and conclude a gold-mining and spice-trading deal; his importance bolstered by a slew of grand titles bestowed upon him by his royal backers, among them 'Admiral of the Ocean Sea, Viceroy of the Indies', and for good measure, 'Governor of all the lands he might discover on his voyage'.[11]

A couple of months later, on 12 October, the lookout on the *Pinta* sighted land. Alas, it was neither Japan nor China, and certainly not the kingdom of Prester John; in fact Colón had arrived in the Bahamas, a picturesque place with naked

[11]   Edwin Williamson, *The Penguin History of Latin America*, p.7

inhabitants but not much in the way of gold or spices. Instead the natives gave him gifts of fruit and dried leaves with a distinctive aroma. The Europeans ate the fruit and threw the leaves overboard; then, hearing of a large island to the south called Colba and deciding that this must be Japan, set sail again, making landfall at what would become the resort of Bariay in the country we know as Cuba. Again, there was precious little gold, but the crew were rewarded by the sight of the local inhabitants walking around with trumpet-sized bundles of burning leaves in their mouths, the same leaves that the Europeans had discarded in the Bahamas, twisted, said one observer, like paper muskets and giving off a fragrant smoke. The locals called these smouldering musket-like bundles *tabacos*, and the leaves with which they were made were known as *cohiba*, *cojiba* or *cohoba*.

Before returning to Spain and his royal patrons with tall tales of the abundant riches of the New World and natives carrying caged parrots, Colón sailed eastwards from Cuba but wrecked his flagship, the *Santa Maria*, on a coral

Cristóbal Colón's flotilla — the Santa Maria, *the* Pinta *and the* Nina

reef off an island that he named La Isla Española, shortened to Hispaniola, the greater part of which is today occupied by the Dominican Republic, the western portion forming Haiti. Using the wreckage of the *Santa Maria*, he built a settlement in what is now Haiti, returning the following year with 70 ships and 1,500 Spaniards only to find that the men he had left behind had been slaughtered. He then built a settlement further east near what today is the Dominican resort and port city of Puerto Plata.

In all, Colón would make four visits to the West Indies, as they became known, touring what would later become the great cigar countries of the region; in addition to Cuba and Hispaniola, his travels took him to Venezuela, Colombia, Jamaica and Honduras. Even after his death he continued to travel to the Caribbean, his remains being shipped first to Santo Domingo on Hispaniola, then to Cuba, before being interred in Seville after Spain's empire shrank from a global concern to a few flyspecks of land in the Atlantic and a couple of tiny North African enclaves.

Columbus may have died, but the age of the cigar had been born. The first European to take up the habit was Rodrigo de Jerez, who apparently smoked a *tabaco* every day, and became so fond of them that he brought some back to Spain with him. However, citizens of his home town, Ayamonte, were so terrified by the sight of smoke issuing from his nostrils and mouth that, not unnaturally, they suspected the work of Satan, and the Inquisition imprisoned the unfortunate explorer for several years.

The fate of Jerez was representative of the mixed reception that greeted tobacco in the Old World, and its introduction across Europe was gradual, seeping rather than flooding out of the Iberian peninsula.

Once it had discovered the New World, Spain did not really know what to do with it other than ship out boatloads of adventurous fortune-hunters and rough, uneducated peasants to populate the islands of Hispaniola and Cuba – or die of disease trying. For two decades the mainland of the Americas remained more or less a mystery to the European settlers on the Caribbean islands, their only knowledge of it coming from raiding parties sent out to capture slaves as the indigenous populations of the islands of Cuba and Hispaniola declined.

It was Hernán Cortés, an ambitious soldier and colonial administrator originally from Extremadura, who, on learning that an official expedition was being equipped in Spain to explore and conquer the mainland, decided that he would like to claim the glory and riches for himself, and set off to topple the Aztecs and establish what he would call New Spain and we today know as Mexico. There is a tale that it was Cortés who in 1518 presented the Spanish king, Charles V, with the first tobacco seeds brought to Europe,

Cortes' fleet

introducing the plant to European agriculture. And as Europeans ventured further into the vast continent, they discovered that tobacco was widely used by the indigenous peoples. Two years later, Hernández de Toledo brought some seeds back to Portugal, and not to be left out, that other great nation of navigators and explorers, Holland, claimed Damien de Goes as the man who brought seeds from Florida to present to King Sebastian of Portugal.

At first tobacco was a curiosity, a strange plant to be pondered by natural philosophers – as scientists were then known – and enjoyed by kings and courtiers. But gradually it became part of European agriculture, and by the second half of the sixteenth century it was being cultivated in France. It is now accepted that it was introduced to French soil by an explorer-priest called André Thévet; however, it was Jean Nicot (whence 'nicotine'), France's ambassador to Portugal, who, returning from Lisbon with some tobacco plants in 1560, promoted its use in court circles as a medicine and a recreational drug. As it spread through Europe, it became increasingly fashionable, and by the time it reached England in the 1570s, the authors of the *Stirpium Adversaria Nova* were ready to ascribe all manner of marvellous properties to the strange-looking plant.

It is usually larger than our comfrey, though found flourishing in the same well-watered spots of rich earth, exposed to the sun. It has very wide leaves, of oblong shape, hairy quality, wider, rounder, larger than those of comfrey ... The stalk grows three cubits high in France, Belgium and England, and very often four or five cubits when it is sown early enough in warmer parts of Aquitaine and Languedoc. It bears flower calyxes in August of a pale, somewhat reddish green ...

For you will observe shipmasters [sailors] *and all others who come back from out there* [i.e., America] *using little funnels, made of palm leaves or straw, in the extreme end of which they stuff* [crumbled dried leaves] *of this plant. This they light, and opening their mouths as much as they can, they suck in the smoke with their breath. By this they say their hunger and thirst are allayed, their strength restored, and their spirits refreshed ... Our age has discovered nothing from the New World which will be numbered among the remedies more valuable and efficacious than this plant for sores, wounds, affections of the throat and chest, and the fever of the plague.*[2]

[2] *Stirpium Adversaria Nova*, trans. Jerome Brooks, in *Tobacco: Its History* (Rosenbach, New York, 1937), Vol. 1, pp.239–40, cited in F. D. Hoeniger and J. F. M. Hoeniger, *The Development of Natural History in Tudor England* (Folger Books, 1969), p.74

Early tobacco cultivation in Cuba

The tobacco first smoked in England came from the British colonies in Virginia and was the harsher *Nicotiana rustica*, a variety that contained huge quantities of nicotine (such is the strength of *Nicotiana rustica* that it is cultivated by gardeners today as an organic pesticide). It was introduced to fashionable society by the adventurer Sir Walter Raleigh and the scientist Thomas Harriot, who is also credited with introducing the pipe in which the leaves were smoked, thus making Britain a pipe-smoking country.

But by the time Sir Walter was perfuming the court of the Virgin Queen with his pipes full of smouldering *Nicotiana rustica*; sophisticated methods of commercial cultivation of tobacco were already being practised in Cuba. According to one historian of Havana cigars, 'Selective plant breeding has been kept throughout history, ever since the first plants of *N. tabacum* were brought to Cuba from Yucatan in 1535 to substitute *N. rustica*.'[3]*Nicotiana tabacum* has a much lower nicotine content than the overpowering variety that was first imported into Cuba.

The early introduction of a different type of tobacco is somewhat at odds with the proud claim in *The World of the Habano*, published by Cuba's Tobacco Research Institute, that 'Every leaf in a Habano is Tabaco Negro Cubano – native Cuban Black Tobacco – directly descended from plants that Columbus first discovered here more than five hundred years ago.'[4]

The truth is that the Europeans were doing what they did best: refining, improving and, as they did not say at the time, adding value to a naturally occurring resource. Although disapproving monarchs, including James I of England, did their best to suppress tobacco use; a little over a century after the sight of the shamanic smoke had perplexed those intrepid arrivals in the New World, it was well established in Europe as a pleasure, a panacea and a business.

'It was in the second half of the sixteenth century that tobacco acquired an economic standing in world commerce and in the agriculture of certain countries, both American and European,' writes Fernando Ortiz in his 1940 book *Cuban Counterpoint*, adding, 'The tobacco of Cuba was raised for the market and was much sought after.'[5]Ortiz argues that along with sugar, tobacco shaped the development of Columbian Cuba.

[3]   Gaspar J. García Galló and Wilfredo Correa García, *The Story of Havana Cigars*, 1st English language translation (Editorial José Martí, Cuba, 2001), pp.32–3

[4]   Mark Brutton, *The World of the Habano*, (Personnel Decisions International, Minneapolis, 2012), Minneapolis, p.18

[5]   Fernando Ortiz, *Cuban Counterpoint*, p.286

Port of Havana, c.1890

The port of Havana became the center for the distri-bution of tobacco because of the circumstance that it was at its roadstead that the Spanish ships assembled with their crews of rowdy sailors and their rich passen-gers for the return trip to the Guadalquivir. For centu-ries Havana was of great importance as the center for the Spanish fleets from Cartagena, Nombre de Dios, Portobello, Vera Cruz, Campeche, and Santo Domingo, all of which gathered in its spacious bay, protected from hurricanes and pirates and situated at the mouth of the Bahama Channel, which was the return route they were obliged to take because of currents and winds. From there these fleets set out in convoy under the protection of the armadas on their way to Seville.[61]

Thus it is due to an accident of geography, the need to assemble sufficiently large convoys to repel the attentions of

[6]   Ibid, p.167

British privateers, and the island's suitability for the cultivation of tobacco that Cuba and its capital Havana emerged as the hub of the global tobacco trade. By now the popularity of tobacco as a luxury product in the Old World was well established, and it was a lucrative source of income that the Spanish crown sought to protect from a well-organised and ingenious smuggling network.

This was no longer a matter of a sailor bringing back a few *tabacos* for himself and his friends; entire shiploads of contraband tobacco were being landed in Holland, France and England, where the habit had really taken off. What is more, the demand from smugglers stimulated the growth of a tobacco-processing industry in Cuba. Officially tobacco could only be exported in leaf form to Spain, where it would then be processed and turned into snuff.

However, illicit traffickers encouraged the construction of the first Cuban snuff mills in the early seventeenth century. As demand and potential profits soared, the illegal tobacco trade became a parallel industry, with entire plantations dedicated to producing tobacco to be smuggled into Europe. Writing of tobacco farming in Cuba during the 1600s, author Adriano Martínez Rius claimed that during the 'second half of the century, all of the tobacco grown in both the Eastern and Central regions was smuggled out of the country'.[7]

As a response to the growing threat from smugglers, Spain tightened its controls on the lucrative trade: anyone discovered trading with foreigners in the precious leaves

[7] Adriano Martínez Rius, *Habano the King* (Epicur, Barcelona, 1999), p.17

Royal Tobacco Factory, Seville

risked death or deportation. And once the tobacco arrived in Spain, the crown was able to exert further controls, with the Spanish government dictating that the raw material exported from the New World was unloaded on the banks of the Guadalquivir, in the docks of Seville.

In 1614, King Philip III had decreed that all tobacco grown in Spain's colonies in the New World should be shipped to Seville. The southern Spanish city was the location of the House of Trade, the government body that regulated relations between Spain and its growing empire overseas. The House of Trade licensed captains, granted permission for voyages of exploration and levied duties on imports such as tobacco. Small factories soon established themselves in the city to make snuff and prepare tobacco for use by Spanish aficionados, and it was in 1676[8] that cigars were first produced there. Even so, these were far from being the cigars with which we are familiar, with the leaf

[8]   Bernard Le Roy and Maurice Szafran, *The Illustrated History of Cigars* (Harold Starke Publishing, 1998), p.4

from the tobacco-cultivating regions of the Caribbean rolled inside leaves taken from other plants that demonstrated the strength and size necessary to contain the precious blend.

Just how valuable the tobacco trade had become was made clear in the early 1700s, when work began on the truly palatial Royal Tobacco Factory in Seville, which was the largest commercial building in eighteenth-century Spain, second only in size to the royal palace of El Escorial. But Spanish prestige and hegemony of the tobacco trade was dented by the British when they occupied Havana between 1762 and 1763, during which time Cuban leaf and seeds found their way to Britain and its colonies, particularly Connecticut.

Before handing the island back to Spain, the British cleaned Cuba out of tobacco leaf, leading to shortages as the capacity of the island to produce was outstripped by the demand from the mother country. With more attractive terms offered by smugglers, this led to something of a crisis in the Spanish tobacco trade. Insufficient quantities and inferior-quality leaf were sent to the royal factory at Seville, and as the popularity of snuff began to wane in favour of cigars, complaints were heard about the quality of the product made in Spanish factories. 'Therefore, cigars coming directly from Cuba through smugglers were the ones preferred in Europe, especially in England,' explains Adriano Martínez Rius.

Cigars were poised on the brink of huge change, as it was also from this time that techniques in leaf handling had advanced sufficiently to enable cigars to be constructed along the modern lines we know today: filler leaves held together by a binder leaf, all clothed in the exquisite wrapper leaf.

The accusation of inferiority of Iberian cigars 'was that those made in Spain consisted of leaves of irregular quality. This was because the Monopoly officers in the Island used to accept any mix of different quality leaves as "first class", whilst the best ones used to be reserved for smugglers. In addition, these leaves of dubious quality fermented during the lengthy journey, acquiring an unpleasant taste. This was not helped by Spanish factories' inclusion of tobacco trimmings, cuttings and scraps in the finished product. These additions impeded the flow of smoke, making smoking less pleasurable.'[9]

And while the densely packed bales of leaves may have been subject to an uncontrolled fermentation over the course of several weeks at sea, it appears that 'the few cigars which arrived from Havana were in perfect condition'.[10] It is said that 'even the King himself was aware of this fact, and he also made his orders of cigars directly from the Island, thus acknowledging the unsurpassable quality of Cuban cigars'.[11]

In 1796, Francisco Cabañas opened the first recorded private cigar factory in Havana, and the closing years of the century saw small cigar manufacturers operating openly in and around the capital, with the official representatives of His Majesty looking on with a well-bribed sightless eye. The hegemony of the Spanish-made cigar was coming to an end, and the age of the Cuban cigar factory was dawning.

In 1817, just over two hundred years since King Philip had decreed that all raw tobacco from the New World be

. . . .

[9] Martínez Rius, *Habano the King,* p.23

[10] Le Roy and Szafran, *The Illustrated History of Cigars,* p.48

[11] Martínez Rius, *Habano the King,* p.23

shipped to Seville, the Spanish tobacco monopoly was abolished. From now on the growers and workshops were free to sell to and make for whomever they liked, and, coinciding with a surge in demand, the Havana cigar business took off.

*   *   *

One of the few upsides of the generation-long struggle against Napoleon was that during the Peninsular War, Britain acquired a taste for cigars. Previously tobacco had been consumed in clay pipes or ground up into snuff and carried round in little jewelled caskets; the celebrated Georgian tea-drinking dandy Lord Petersham once observed with due solemnity that a light-blue Sèvres snuffbox may well have been 'a nice summer box, but would not do for winter wear'. However, soldiers returning from the continent brought cigars with them, and in order to meet the demand, cigars began to be made in factories in England.

Stripping leaves in a Victorian London cigar factory

Domestic production, duties levied on imports and of course smuggling meant that at first, numbers of officially imported cigars were small: in 1823, for instance, just 1,950 cigars were imported into the UK. It was also in 1823 that Byron wrote *The Island*; he was clearly a terrific ambassador for the cigar, as in the following year, an estimated 1,153,500 cigars were imported, while by 1830, the year William IV ascended the throne, that figure had risen to just over 19 million.[12]

The picture was more or less the same across the rest of Europe, and in North America too, where in 1800 the young nation had welcomed the new century by electing a tobacco farmer called Thomas Jefferson to the presidency, and where a later occupant of the White House, Ulysses S. Grant would consume 20 cigars a day.

The great nineteenth-century cigar boom was under way, and by the middle years of the century, the modern top-hatted Victorian gentleman was consuming his tobacco in tubular form. Isambard Kingdom Brunel, arguably the most forward-looking man of his day, daring to invent and build such contraptions as would have been unimaginable even in Byron's day, was one of the cigar's most powerful advocates.

The most remarkable expression of this modern age was the Great Exhibition of the Works of Industry of all Nations of 1851, which took place in a glittering palace of glass and cast iron that towered above the treeline of London's Hyde Park.

Conceived by His Royal Highness Prince Albert, Queen Victoria's husband and Prince Consort, the Great Exhibition

[12] Figures supplied by Hunters & Frankau

The Great Exhibition, London, 1851

was a showcase for all that was modern and marvellous about the world in the middle of the nineteenth century. Among the exhibits that dazzled visitors were the fabled Koh-i-Noor diamond; a stuffed elephant carrying a maharajah's howdah; a folding piano; an expandable hearse; a floating church; a pulpit that used rubber tubes to connect the preacher to parishioners who were hard of hearing; Mr Colt's patented revolving cylinder firearm; Patek Philippe's keyless watch, and a glass casket of Cabañas cigars.

Cabañas, it will be remembered, was the name of the first recorded cigar factory owner, and the Cabañas brand, recorded at Havana's trademark office in 1810, had become extremely popular, especially in Britain. The importance of branding had been grasped rapidly by cigar makers in Cuba, and by the time of the Great Exhibition, many of the brands still known today were already in existence, among them Por Larrañaga (1834), Punch (1840), H. Upmann (1844), Partagás (1845), El Rey del Mundo (1848) and Romeo y

Julieta (1850). From humble beginnings in small rustic work-shops or farmhouses near the plantations, the factories in which these cigars were made were increasingly impressive structures, the best-known surviving example of which is the Partagás factory, with the cheeky legend *Real Fábrica de Tabacos* emblazoned across its facade – a reminder that the crown of cigar making had passed from Seville to Havana. As the nineteenth century progressed, connoisseurs spoke increasingly of Havanas rather than Sevillas.

By the middle of the nineteenth century, Havana had emerged as the cigar capital of the world. In 1859, the city boasted a staggering 1,295 cigar factories and a further 38 factories making cigarettes, with the industry providing employment for 15,000 workers.[13] The second half of the century saw a consolidation and greater indus-trial concentration of the manufacturing of cigars; with the booming cigar industry, the later nineteenth century saw

----

[13] García Galló and Correa García, *The Story of Havana Cigars*, p.38

Stamp commemorating Manuel de Céspedes and the centenary of the Ten Years' War

a corresponding rise in aspirations for Cuban independence, as Spain's empire in the Americas disintegrated. On 10 October 1868, a disgruntled Creole landowner called Carlos Manuel de Céspedes issued a proclamation of independence, starting a struggle known as the Ten Years' War.

The war may have provided the heroic backstory for the dreams of Cuban independence, but it played havoc with agriculture, including tobacco cultivation in the east of the country. The ruin of farmers, particularly sugar farmers, enabled the American purchase of farmland, a process of financial colonisation described by one historian as an 'economic invasion', which accelerated at the end of the century when ever-simmering nationalist sentiment led and articulated by the revolutionary poet José Martí flared into a conflict that would engulf the entire country, alarming America to such an extent that it too went to war with Spain, delivering the *coup de grâce* that would push the creaking old colonial power from the world stage.

The war devastated the economy, and yet when hostilities ceased, Cuba had little to show for it. The peace treaty between Spain and the USA imposed a military government on the island in order to rebuild its shattered economy and infrastructure, meaning that in essence, Cuba was as independent as the United States allowed it to be. When the American forces left in 1902, the USA retained a military base at Guantanamo and also the right to intervene in Cuban affairs should it feel it necessary for the 'maintenance of a government adequate for the protection of life, property and individual liberties'.[14]

Increasingly the property needing protection was American. What was a calamity for many Cuban cigar makers was an opportunity for foreign interests to buy into Cuba. British investment had first begun in Havana in the late 1880s, and as the British consul stressed in 1890, the fact that his country's interest was strictly commercial was appreciated by local businesses. 'It would be regarded favorably by the Spanish and the Cubans,' he observed, 'because they understood that the interests of Great Britain are of a purely commercial character and the development can, therefore, tend only to the preservation of the social order and security of property.'[15]

At that time, the appetite for cigars in America was voracious. It is today a truism to talk of 'big tobacco', but then tobacco was huge. This was the era of J.B. Duke's Tobacco Trust. 'At the turn of the nineteenth century, America's favorite tobacco product was unquestionably the cigar, and consumers spent more money for cigars than for cigarettes, snuff, chewing and smoking leaf combined.'[16]

---

[14] Quoted in Williamson, *The Penguin History of Latin America*, p.439

[15] Quoted in Jean Stubbs, *Tobacco on the Periphery* (Cambridge University Press, 1985), p.22

[16] Maurice Duke and Daniel P. Jordan, *Tobacco Merchant: The Story of Universal Leaf Tobacco Company* (University Press of Kentucky, Kentucky, 2014), p.53

The expanding American market

Domestic production in thousands of factories across the nation rose from an already impressive four billion cigars in 1890 to a staggering seven billion by 1906. And as well as being grown domestically, one of the chief sources of leaf for these cigars was, of course, Cuba.

At the turn of the century, English company Henry Clay and Gustavo Bock took control of a number of Cuban factories and 35 cigar brands. At the same time, businesses from America, which was already Cuba's largest trading partner, acquired not just a dozen Cuban factories and 149 brands, but also plantations to supply leaf tobacco to the numerous cigar factories on the American mainland. Henry Clay and Bock would also become American-owned, with eponym Bock becoming tobacco tycoon Buck Duke's right-hand man in Havana. Local manufacturers were, understandably, concerned at this 'consolidation' and at the rising exports in leaf tobacco to the US.

In the early years of the twentieth century the tensions between the remaining independents and the mighty Trust turned to open hostility when Bock published a book claiming that he had devoted his 46 years in Cuba to improving the manufacture of cigars, and that those cigars made in the factories under his direction 'cannot be equaled in Aroma, quality and manufacture by any other cigar in the world'.[17] Rather like the pamphlet wars of sixteenth- and seventeenth-century Britain, the following year the independents retaliated with a publication of their own, claiming that 'nobody considers Mr Bock to be an able manager of cigar factories'.

Given all the upheaval, cigar makers in Cuba can be forgiven for not paying a great deal of attention to the decision taken in 1903 by Eduardo León Jimenes, whose family had been farming tobacco since 1880, to open a small factory employing three rollers. It was not the size of the operation that was significant but rather its location. It was not in Havana; it was not even in Cuba: Jimenes' factory was in the rich and fertile tobacco-growing Cibao valley in the Dominican Republic.

As Hispaniola, the island had been first settled by Columbus, but its former grandeur, testified to by the splendid cathedral in Santo Domingo, was a long-distant memory. If anything, the Dominican Republic had had an even more violent nineteenth century than had Cuba. Sharing the island uneasily with the neighbouring nation of Haiti, it had only won its independence after fighting the Haitians, the French, the Spanish and factions within its own borders. It entered the twentieth century bankrupt, and economically reliant on the USA, which felt, as in Cuba, that its troops and its businesses could come and go as they

---

[17] Quoted in Stubbs, *Tobacco on the Periphery*, p.31

pleased. The Dominican Republic had long been a supplier of tobacco leaf for export, with the native Olor Dominicano producing an aromatic tobacco; but by the late nineteenth century the first factory had appeared in the town of Santiago de los Caballeros. A new phase in the commercial life of the country was beginning. Jimenes' little enterprise would in time prosper and grow to become a substantial business. Rather appropriately, Jimenes christened his factory La Aurora (the dawn).

In Havana, meanwhile, the dawn of Cuba as a self-determining sovereign state that had been promised by the election as president of Tomás Estrada Palma proved false. In 1906 the Americans once more imposed direct rule through a governor. Even though self-government was re-established in 1909, over the next dozen or so years, American troops continued to be sent to the island to protect life, liberty and the ever-increasing amount of American-owned property.

As the twentieth century progressed, the pace of American investment accelerated: in a single decade, between 1914 and 1923, 'US investment in the Cuban economy increased sixfold'.[18] And just as the American military government of the island had improved its infrastructure, so the tsunami of US investment brought new scientific methods of production, chief among which was the development of a disease-resistant strain of tobacco called Habanensis, which first appeared in 1907. In 1941 this was superseded by the improved Criollo, from which the Corojo strain was developed expressly for the growing of wrappers.

....

[18] Williamson, *The Penguin History of Latin America*, p.440

These have been adapted over time; Criollo 98 and Corojo 99, for example, have a higher yield and increased resistance to blue mould.

By the beginning of the 1920s, it was not just the cigars that were drawing Americans to Havana. Cuba became particularly attractive to those Americans keen to avoid the restrictions imposed upon them by Congressman Volstead's National Prohibition Act, which, officially at least, turned American into an alcohol-free nation from 1920 until 1933.

The lasting legacy of this unpopular piece of legislation was the establishment of organised crime in the United States, and when the source of income afforded by the sale

Prohibition

Prohibition-era speakeasy membership cards

of illegal liquor was withdrawn, this sophisticated criminal network was keen to explore new business opportunities. By fortunate coincidence, the year that Prohibition was repealed, Cuba underwent one of its periodic political convulsions with the so-called Sergeants' Revolt; and the end of 1933 saw an American accountant coming to visit a Cuban army typist in Havana. This, however, was no dull meeting of clerical staff.

At just over one and a half metres in height, Meyer Lansky was too short even to be dubbed the Napoleon of Crime. Instead he became known as the Mob's Accountant. His host was Sergeant Batista, a former military stenographer who would emerge as the strongman dictator of Cuba. In 1933, these two men forged an agreement that for the next quarter of a century would see them run the island less as a sovereign state and more as a private business. Lansky came away with the lucrative gambling rights. Money laundering, drug trafficking, prostitution and so forth would soon follow, and within a few years, he and his associates had turned Havana into what was variously known as 'the Paris of the Caribbean' and 'the most dazzling brothel in the Americas'.[19]

[19]   Enrique Cirules, *The Empire of Havana* (Editorial José Martí, 2003), p.41

This is the period of Cuban history most mythologised in America: a time of large American cars, cigars, cabaret, sun, sex, roulette and rum. With easier air travel, Cuba seemed closer than ever to the USA. Evening flights from Palm Beach would disgorge planeloads of sybarites in evening dress who would carouse and gamble until the rays of the rising sun called them back to the airport for their return flight.

For those who wanted to stay on, there were thousands of rooms in luxury hotels that sprang up during the 1950s. Some – like the Capri, where George Raft used to hold court; the Havana Hilton, renamed the Habana Libre; and the Riviera, a monument to late-fifties luxury kitsch, frozen for half a century – remain to testify to the darkly glamorous decadence of the period.

Of course it did not last. By 1959, the jewelled women and dinner-jacketed men had disappeared from the streets of Havana to be replaced by battle dress and beards as Dr Castro's triumphant revolution swept Sergeant Batista and his mafia cronies off the island.

In the iconography of elitism, few symbols are as powerful as a flaunted cigar, and in the late 1950s the cigar industry in Havana symbolised the exploitation of working people by factory owners who in many cases were not even Cuban. In the eyes of the revolutionary government it was a

Castro, Sierra Mastre forest, 1958

wrong that needed righting, and '137 days after the revolutionary triumph of January 1st 1959',[20] or 17 May 1959, as it was known in the rest of the world, the first Agrarian Reform Law was passed, the initial step on the path to full nationalisation of foreign property in August of the following year.

....

[20] Martínez Rius, *Habano the King*, p.99

As it happened, the cigar factories were not nationalised; they were 'intervened'. Adriano Martínez Rius defines this process of intervention as meaning 'that the management of the factories was transferred to the State – thus appointing a comptroller who would be in charge of managing those factories, once most of them had been abandoned by their owners'.[21] However, as the experiences of some of those who had not yet fled the country would show, the line that divided intervened property from nationalised property was not particularly distinct. Interviewed for the magazine *Cigar Aficionado* in 1994, Manuel Quesada, a member of a dynasty that had been in the tobacco business in Cuba since the 1880s, recalled the way he and his family were forced to leave their home and their business:

> *Four guys in a jeep with machine guns came to the door, asked for the keys to the safe, sealed it and one said: 'This vault has been intervened by the government; nobody can touch it.'*
>
> *In August of 1960, my brother and I were sent to Miami, and* [the following month] *my mother and two sisters came. My father spent a year educating Castro's men on how to run his business. One day they told him: 'Go. Don't come back.'*

But Castro's men were not about to stop at merely redistributing land, nationalising businesses and 'intervening' cigar factories. There is a persistent and often-repeated rumour that the very concept of the Cuban cigar itself

---

[21] Ibid.

Fidel Castro, enjoying a cigar in 1974

was to be revolutionised. According to this story, brands were considered counter-revolutionary, all right for the bourgeoisie in a 'running-dog lackey of the capitalist imperialist system' sort of way, but hardly the stuff that dreams were made of in the brave new world being conjured up by the tropical Prospero Fidel Castro. Individual cigar brands, he announced, were 'a thing of the past'.[22]

With this rhetorical flourish the great orator consigned 140 years of Havana heritage to the dustbin of history: among the brands that died in 1959 was the historic Cabañas, the first Cuban cigar marque and the representative of Cuba's cigar industry at the Great Exhibition 108 years earlier.

In Batista's day, there had been almost a thousand different types of Havana cigar on the market. The revolution decreed that in future there would be just four sizes of one brand, called Siboney, which had hitherto only been available to the domestic market. In addition, these cigars would be stripped of their colourful raiment: there would be

[22] Le Roy and Szafran, *The Illustrated History of Cigars*, p.62

no bands and no brightly coloured images plastered over the boxes. Just as the drab olive colour of army fatigues filled the streets of Havana with a sartorial equality, so from now on all cigars would be indistinguishable from one another.

But history subsequently followed a different path, and if his biographer is to be believed, one of the men who played an important role in averting the implementation of this suicidal edict was Zino Davidoff, a Geneva cigar merchant.

Davidoff, who continued to have close ties with Cuba, warned about these developments. He urged the Cubans to abandon actions of this kind already underway and to retain the established brands. The brands' appeal and aura could be beneficial, such as attributes connected with names like Romeo y Julieta and Partagás, Hoyo de Monterrey and Bolívar.

Davidoff's advice gradually changed the minds of the new managers. In the end, the Caribbean island shelved the Siboney idea. [23]

[23] Dieter H. Wirtz, *Davidoff: Legend – Myth – Reality* (Econ Verlag, Berlin, 2006), p.160

Although the Siboney brand was revived in 1988, when the Austrian tobacco monopoly marketed a brand of cigarillo made from Cuban tobacco, the idea that Siboney was indeed going to replace all cigar brands is today regarded with scepticism. When directly questioned about the proposal in 1994, thirty or so years after the idea was supposed to have been thought up, Fidel Castro was adamant: 'That would have been insanity! That would have been crazy. I always wanted them to create new brands.'[24]

If the idea had ever been considered, it was never put into action; instead, a new product was created when the Cuban authorities honoured Davidoff by naming a brand of cigar after him:

Perhaps out of gratefulness, perhaps as a sign of respect, Cubatabaco proposed to the Geneva tobacco trader in 1967 that it produce a Havana brand under his name in Cuba, to his specification of course. One year later, in 1968, the first Havanas under the Davidoff label were launched on the market: the Davidoff No.1, the Davidoff No.2 and the Ambassadrice. A new era had begun.[25]

And not just in Cuba. For a while, there were those who thought that Castro would stay in power for a year or two. The Bay of Pigs, Kennedy's trade embargo, the Cuban missile crisis and increased superpower tension in the Caribbean put an end to such hopes.

[24] Marvin R. Shanken, 'A Conversation with Fidel', *Cigar Aficionado*, Summer 1994

[25] Wirtz, *Davidoff*, p.160

As the embargo placed on trade with Cuba by President Kennedy began to hit the cigar business in the US, the popularity of cigars from other Central American and Caribbean tobacco-growing nations increased. Firms such as La Aurora in the Dominican Republic, now a well-established business, were ideally placed to capitalise on this blow to the Cuban cigar business. And it was not solely being denied access to what had been traditionally its largest market that affected the Cuban cigar industry: the early 1960s saw a brain drain of tobacco experts away from Havana, a diaspora that gave new vigour to cigar making elsewhere. It was at this time that the Dominican Republic acquired its second main tobacco variety, the Piloto Cubano, which began as Cuban seeds brought to the country by those fleeing the revolution.

Nor was the loss of many talented industry figures the only ill to afflict Cuba's post-revolution cigar business. Between 1959 and 1989, 'tobacco's share in total exports [from Cuba] shrank from 9 to 1·6 percent'. [26] And at the end of the 1970s, production crashed. 'One reason was the decline in tobacco leaf production (from 52,000 to 8,000 tons in 1976–80) due to blue mold [sic],' writes political and economic analyst Irving Louis Horowitz. [27]

Elsewhere in the region, the 1970s and 1980s saw the establishment of new cigar-making centres, and the renaissance of old ones. In Honduras, for example, the tradition of working with tobacco reached back to the late eighteenth century, when the Spanish state created a royal tobacco

[26] Irving Louis Horowitz (ed.), *Cuban Communism, 1959–1995*
        (8th edition, Transaction Publishers, New Brunswick, 1995), p.205

[27] Ibid.

factory there, in effect a more architecturally modest New World branch of the sprawling Seville site. Almost two hundred years later, in the 1970s, it was to Honduras that Davidoff turned to make a range of cigars to sell in the US.

Brazil, Ecuador, Nicaragua, Jamaica and Mexico were among the other nations to benefit from this shift in the balance of cigar power. However, the most dramatic effect was in the Dominican Republic, which as the neighbouring island to Cuba shared similar meteorological, geological and botanical characteristics. Dominican cigars began to be exported to Miami in the mid-1960s. This trickle became a tsunami in the 1970s when the Dominican government set up 'free zones' where the building of cigar factories was encouraged with tax incentives. The first free zone opened in 1969 in La Romana in the south-east of the island rather than in the traditional tobacco-cultivating country, and it was where Consolidated (Tabacalera de García) relocated from the Canary Islands. The arrival of such a major producer sent a strong message that the Dominican Republic was open for business.

Attracted by political stability, the benevolent financial climate and ideal tobacco-cultivating conditions, another large American cigar company, General Cigar, also opened facilities on the island, but this time in the free zone of Santiago. And it was in the Dominican Republic that American giants made non-Cuban versions of classic marques, including Partagás, Upmann and Montecristo.

After the devastation of the second half of the 1970s, the situation of the Cuban cigar industry improved, but the early 1990s saw it hit by a crisis every bit as worrying as blue mould. On the evening of 9 November 1989, remarkable scenes appeared on television screens around the world as thousands of East Germans swarmed through checkpoints along the Berlin Wall and with primitive tools, or just their bare hands, began spontaneously to demolish the most concrete symbol, figuratively and physically, of the Cold War. Thereafter the pace of events quickened. It took barely 18 months for the once mighty Soviet Union to fragment.

This catastrophic loss of its chief sponsor affected every aspect of life in Cuba, and its effect on the cigar industry was magnified by an announcement the following year. 'In 1990, the international tobacco firm Davidoff et Cie ended its dealings with Cuba, alleging a deterioration in the quality of Cuba's products, and started manufacturing cigars with tobacco grown in other Caribbean countries. This was a serious blow to Cuba.'[28] But with or without Davidoff, the cigar continued to be a central pillar of the Cuban economy, as Castro confirmed in an interview in 1994.

It is one of our most important export items. It is also one of our main sources of revenue. It is also an important factor for us in the domestic market. In addition to that, we have the hard currency which comes from exporting cigars. Cigars are one of the four or five most important items of export that we have. First, it's sugar, then nickel, fish, tourism. These are the main items that provide revenues. Biotechnology is gaining ground as well as the pharmaceutical industry. And now cigars are more or less in fifth place. Historically it has been very important.[29]

. . . .

[28] Ibid.

[29] Shanken, 'A Conversation with Fidel', *Cigar Aficionado*, Summer 1994

The departure of Davidoff, while a blow to Cuba, was to spark a bonanza in the Dominican Republic, which received the ultimate benediction when the business moved its production to the Cibao valley. Dr Ernst Schneider, who had bought Davidoff in the early 1970s, was adamant that only total control over every aspect of the cigars bearing the company's name would ensure the long-term stability of his business and the quality and consistency his customers demanded.

Zino Davidoff and Dr Ernst Schneider

As the brand's advertising of the time declared, Cuban Davidoffs had come to be regarded as *le summum* (the ultimate), a reputation that accounts for the astonishing prices vintage Havana Davidoffs continue to command over a quarter of a century after the last one was rolled. But in spite of, or maybe because of, this success, Cuba announced that El Laguito (known colloquially in Europe as the Davidoff factory) would be dedicated to the new Cohiba line that would soon become commercially available.

Cohiba of course became a magical name too, but in being forced to relocate its production elsewhere in

the Caribbean, Davidoff found itself in the right place at the right time as the cigar boom of the 1990s ignited. Smoking legislation was far less restrictive than today and a cigar became something of a fashion accessory, brandished by celebrities as diverse as Demi Moore, Sean Combs, Linda Evangelista, Arnold Schwarzenegger, Madonna, Jack Nicholson, Beyoncé, JLo and Jay Z. Demand soared, particularly in the United States, and non-Cuban cigars benefited worldwide from the troubles of the Cuban cigar industry as it adjusted to life after the Soviet Union, when both pests and shortages of such basic commodities as string badly affected harvests. By the end of the century the Dominican Republic was selling more than 200 million cigars a year, with the famous La Romana factory said to be working three shifts around the clock to meet demand.

Eventually, obeying the rules of all bubble markets since tulip mania gripped the Netherlands in the early seventeenth century, cigar consumption plateaued and then dropped. But it did not collapse completely and has grown more sustainably during the early twenty-first century. The Dominican Republic remains the largest single producer of what I suppose are called premium cigars, but the most explosive growth in recent years has been in Nicaragua, which has pushed Cuba's annual production of around 85 million cigars into third place. These countries emerge as the leaders against a backdrop of growth in high-quality tobacco cultivation and cigar making across the region.

Now, with relations between Cuba and the United States entering a new phase, the cigar world stands poised on the brink of change once again.

GROWING & MAKING

Cigars are often likened to wines, not least for the ritual and snobbery around them, and like wines they begin life as a simple agricultural product like any other, a seed germinating in the soil – the rich soil found in the fertile areas of the Caribbean and Central American cigar-making nations: the Real and Cibao valleys of the Dominican Republic; Estelí and Jalapa in Nicaragua; and of course the legendary Vuelta Abajo of Cuba.

Pinar del Rio, Vuelta Abajo

These landscapes are dramatic, majestic and give the impression of having survived unchanged from the days of prehistory. To arrive in the Vuelta Abajo shortly after dawn, the mist still draping itself over a landscape punctured here and there by the serrated profile of palm fronds, while above rise the verdant hills, sparkling emerald-like in the morning light, is to experience this landscape much as it was not merely centuries ago, but in aeons past.

As has always been the case, cultivation of cigar tobacco remains a laborious business: a Cuban *veguero* (farmer) may have half a million plants in his care, each of which will need to be visited approximately 150 times through its life. The process begins with the preparation of the land during the steamy summer months. Fields are often tilled with bullock-drawn ploughs; the expense of intensive farming equipment aside, the weight of the animal-drawn plough is less likely to compact the soil.

Planting begins in September and lasts for several weeks. As the miracle of germination transforms seeds into plants, the tobacco seedlings are cosseted. In the old days, young plants were protected by a covering of straw; today, when they first poke their shoots through the loose rich soil, they find themselves in little seed trays in greenhouses, or sheltered under plastic tunnels in the fields.

Once the plants have grown to about a foot in height (this takes around 45 days), they are planted out in the fields. After 10 days or so, those plants destined to become wrappers have a translucent ceiling of cheesecloth placed high above them, which diffuses the powerful tropical sunlight as they grow. Entire tobacco fields resemble large marquees, the sun-bleached fabric contrasting with the lush green of the plump leaves sprouting beneath. This shade-grown plant is taller and produces larger leaves in greater numbers than the sun-grown tobacco that comprises the filler and contributes the majority of the flavour to the cigar.

Seedlings

With sufficient sunlight and water the plants grow rapidly, and as soon as there is the first sign of a flower, about 45 days after transplanting from tray to field [*see* page 81], the farmer snaps off the top bud and any side shoots to stimulate the leaf growth below. After another 15 days or so, harvesting can begin. This is not a single picking, but a process that can last a month from when the first leaf is picked, as, at intervals of several days, small numbers of leaves, no more than three or four at a time, are removed, working from the bottom up, leaving the smaller leaves at the top, the *ligero* – those closest to the sun, with the highest nicotine content and greatest amount of flavour – till last.

As they grow taller, reaching the height of a man, shade-grown plants require more pickings. Then, as the bullock carts burdened with piles of leaves secured under tarpaulins rumble slowly out of the fields, if the climate permits, a late crop is planted and the whole exhausting, back-breaking process begins again.

Cultivating sun-grown leaves for filler

The bullock carts bearing their precious cargo of flavoursome leaves do not have to travel far; their destination is the curing barn, hundreds of which punctuate the landscape. These used to be rudimentary thatched buildings with stamped-earth floors, and even now they tend towards simplicity: a tall, steeply pitched corrugated metal roof over crudely fashioned wooden walls.

The leaves are sorted according to plumpness and size, bound together and hung over poles that are hoisted into racks in the barn. As the leaves dry and the green begins to turn to an autumnal yellow-brown, they are moved higher up into the eaves of the barn while newer arrivals take their place on the lower rungs. Some leaves may stay here for six weeks until they are judged ready to continue their journey.

The sight of a curing barn is a memorable one. The visual image is of a church full of kippers that have been dip-dyed to achieve a perfect gradation of colour from green to brown, while the air is perfumed with the pungent aroma

Curing barn

of young tobacco. Air curing is a skilled business, with plenty of windows and shutters in the walls to guide the flow of air depending on the wind direction.

There is also the less bucolically romantic but rather more effective method of curing that I first encountered in Cuba around the turn of the century. Called the *calfrisa*, it creates a temperature-, ventilation- and humidity-controlled environment in which leaves can be cured predictably, more effectively and more rapidly than in a traditional barn, and given the expense and technical nature of the equipment, it is mostly used to prepare the valuable and delicate wrapper leaf. A crude analogy would be comparing the charm of cooking over an open fire with the convenience of using a fan-assisted oven.

From the curing barns, the tobacco is taken to the *escogida* (sorting house), where the leaves are sorted according to strength, and the *despalillo* (stripping house), where the thickest part of the central vein is removed.

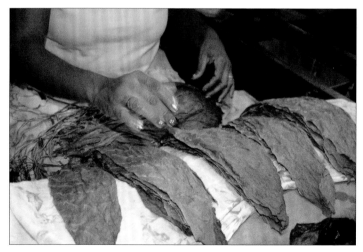

Stripping

Sometimes a poorly made cigar is hard or impossible to draw upon; frequently such a 'plugged' cigar is the result of leaves that have been poorly stripped, allowing the remaining veins to harden until they resemble twigs and creating a blockage that no amount of energetic inhalation can overcome.

The *despalillo* is often just a simple brick building, characterised not so much by its architecture as by the biting tang of ammonia in the air and the tobacco piled in mounds on the floor, into which rapier-like thermometers are thrust. These thermometers are vital to controlling the fermentation procedure, and when the temperature at the core of the pile rises above 42 degrees, it is broken up and rebuilt in reverse.

In common with wine, a period of carefully managed fermentation is vital to achieving the character, consistency and flavour that the connoisseur expects; it may be an ugly term, but this part of the long journey from seed to ash is like a sauna in which the tobacco leaves sweat out impurities. It is during fermentation that the nicotine content is lowered.

Checking fermenting leaves

Again, due to its delicacy, wrapper leaf receives special treatment and is fermented just once, after which it is sorted, graded and then, after a period of resting, baled and allowed to age. The more robustly flavoured and textured sun-grown tobaccos are fermented twice, in the case of the lower and lighter-flavoured *volado* leaves; and thrice for the *seco* leaves from the middle of the plant and the *ligero*, with the final fermentation of the *ligero* and *medio tiempo* leaves (in Cuba, the two top and most powerful leaves of the tobacco plant) taking anything up to 90 days. Leaves from the upper part of the plant are thicker, burn more slowly, hold more flavour and require more fermentation.

'The top leaves are strong for two different reasons,' explains Davidoff's Henke Kelner. 'At the top of the plant they receive more sun, and there is more photosynthesis. Second, even though you have carried out the topping [removal of the flowers and buds] and harvested the other leaves the root is continuing to grow, so in the end you have a plant with just four leaves, with a big root, and all the nutrients go to those four leaves.'[1]

As they rest between fermentations, the leaves are repeatedly aired and moistened; it is the presence of water that catalyses the fermentation process, and if they are damp, the leaves are less likely to tear while being handled.

After their final fermentation, the filler leaves are baled in hessian and labelled to indicate year of baling, strength, size, type of leaf and the stripping and sorting house at which they were processed – all information that will be of use when it comes to blending the leaves to create

[1]   Henke Kelner, interview with the author, June 2016

the specific character expected of the brand and size. They are then left to age, with the strongest leaves requiring the longest period of maturation: in Cuba, this is at least two years for *ligero* and *medio tiempo*.

*   *   *

I have visited a great many factories, manufacturing objects as diverse as watches and shotguns, but no matter what is being made, there is one characteristic that is shared by all good factory visits: if I depart with renewed respect for the product and come away wondering just how they manage to sell it so cheaply, then the day has not been wasted. Never mind how many cigar factories I visit, I am always left with this feeling.

Cigar rolling as it is practised at the highest level – i.e. the creation of hand-made long-filler cigars – has changed little since Byron's day. The air of a cigar factory does not echo to the clank of machinery, the clatter of the assembly line and the roar of the furnace. That does not mean that it is not noisy; for instance, when an important guest visits the *galera* (production floor) in which the *torce-dores* (rollers) sit surrounded by their tools and piles of leaf, the workers will beat their *chavetas* (the distinctive handleless knife with the curved cutting edge) against their benches in a tattoo of welcome, and in some of the more traditional factories, rollers are read to as they work by a lector or reader: in the morning it is the newspaper, and in the afternoon a novel chosen by vote (whence perhaps the name Montecristo).

Arriving in their bales from the country, the leaves are unpacked and inspected. Wrapper leaves, which have not been stripped of their stems, are moistened. In the old days in Cuba I have seen this done by a man in a string vest, his trousers tucked into rubber boots, directing a hosepipe at a handful of about four dozen leaves, after which he would theatrically shake off the excess moisture and move on to the next bunch. These days it is more likely that bundles of these precious caramel- and chocolate-coloured leaves will be hooked onto a rack and placed in a glass-walled moistening room, where they pass through a fine mist of water. They are then sent on to be stripped and graded by size and colour.

Bales of leaves being unpacked at the factory

Stripping and sorting

This task tends to be carried out by women, who sit like casino croupiers within a three-sided or horseshoe-shaped structure with piles of leaves on their laps.

The central stem is removed with a dexterous whip of the hand and the leaf, now in two halves, is placed among its fellows of differing sizes and gradations of colour fanned out around them. In the Dominican Republic, leaves are hand-fed into a machine with roughly the dimensions of an old-fashioned pedal-powered sewing machine, which removes the central stem.

Filler, meanwhile, is unpacked and allowed to rest before the *ligador* (blender) gets to work making up and tasting the blend, and assigning each roller sufficient tobacco to make a day's production.

If the skill of the *ligador* resides in his brain and palate, that of the *torcedor* is in his fingertips. Using few tools – *chaveta*, guillotine, mould and pot of gum – the roller turns a handful of dead leaves into an exquisite instrument of pleasure. The leaves are arranged as they grow on the plant, with the stronger part of the leaf at the mouth (stalk) end, then folded like an accordion or made into little tubes (*entubado*) with the *ligero* at the centre. These tubed or concertinaed leaves are rolled into the binder, the first covering of the filler, and then placed in a mould and pressed for about an hour so that the shape holds while the wrapper is applied. Finally the head of the cigar, which will be clipped, is closed with a little cap of wrapper secured with a tiny dab of gum and just the tension of the wrapper leaf to hold everything in place. It is a miracle of manual dexterity that takes place numerous times throughout the day.

Rolling

Draw testing

The steps sound simple enough, but this is the crucial point in the construction process. Incorrectly stripped leaf can form blockages, as can overfilling, and then the cigar, however excellent the tobacco, is unsmokable. Underfilling is also a problem, and can be seen in the declivities on the side of the cigar. At its most extreme I have folded some cigars to almost 90 degrees, and these pockets of air lead to uneven burning once lit.

To combat these failings, draw machines are sometimes seen (and on occasion even used) in Cuba, and are almost universal in the better-resourced factories around the region. The bunch – i.e. the filler leaves, surrounded by binder – is removed from the mould and placed in a metal tube connected to a source of suction, and the amount of suction needed to draw air through is registered on a dial, on which the acceptable tolerances are marked. In Cuba, this

Ageing

has resulted in a noticeable reduction in problems with draw in recent years. Cigars are also measured to see that they are of the required length and ring gauge, and a representative sample is tasted in a small room lined with cubicles in which sit workers who job it is to assess and provide written ratings of the draw, the combustibility, the aroma, the flavour, the strength, the formation of the ash and the overall quality.

The cigars are then left to age. The champagne houses have their vast caverns hewn from the chalk subsoil; cognac houses have their historic *chaix*; and the great names of Burgundy and Bordeaux boast their atmospheric centuries-old cellars. Cigar factories have their *escaparates*: treasure rooms piled high with finished cigars stacked on cedar shelves and allowed to mature.

Having been introduced to each other on the roller's bench, the flavours of the different leaves take time to

Colour sorting

harmonise, and, kept between 16 and 18 degrees Celsius and at a controlled relative humidity of between 65 and 70 per cent, that is what now happens.

After a while, the cigars are roused from their slumber to be colour-graded, another fabulous piece of the theatre of cigar making. An *escogedor*, or sorter, stands at a vast table with hundreds of cigars in front of him; his job is to place them into similar colour groups, ranging from dark aubergine to honey. A second *escogedor* then arranges each group from dark to light and selects the face upon which the band should be read. The cigars are then banded and boxed, with the colour running from dark to light left to right, so that when the box is opened, the colour variations are almost imperceptible.

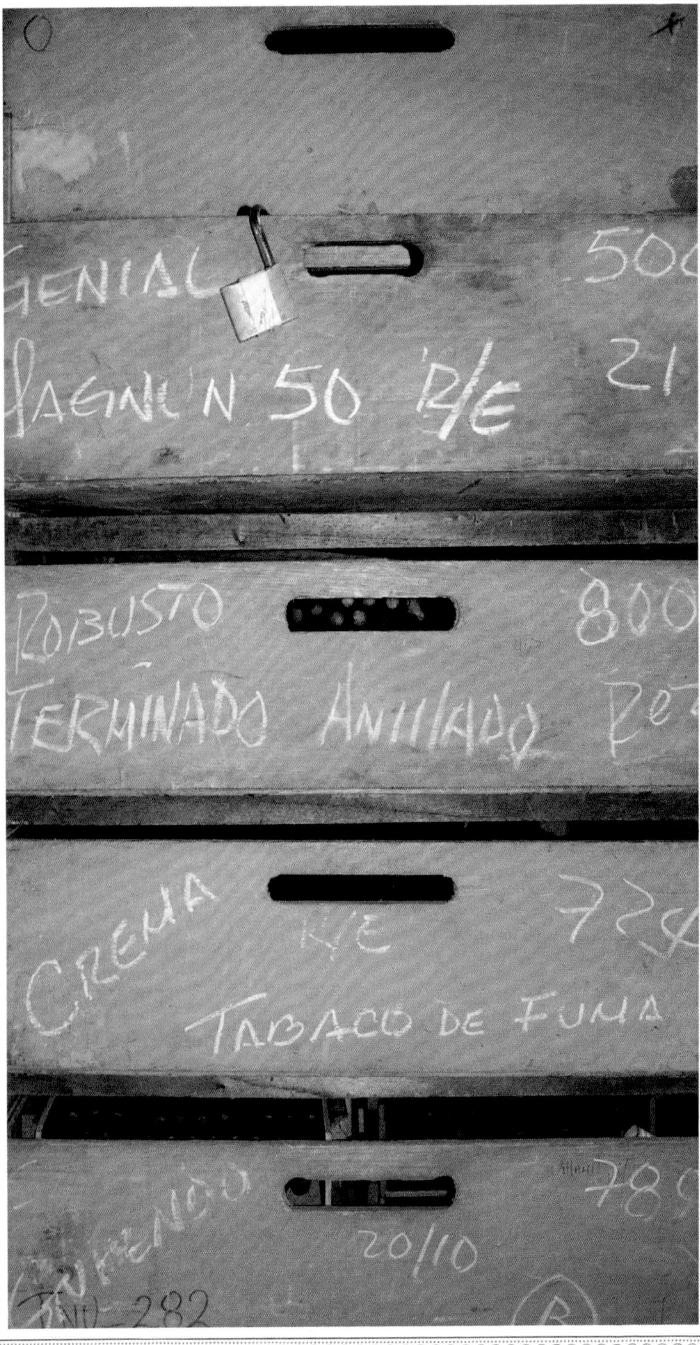
ROBUSTO
TERMINADO ANILLADO
CREMA
TABACO DE FUMA
20/10

LEXICON

ACCORDION

[*See*: *BUNCHING*, page 74]

BANDS

I am rather nostalgic for the days when cabinet-quality cigars were shipped in bundles of 25 and 50, with the only clue to their identity being the yellow ribbon that bound them and the name of the marque hot-stamped onto the sliding lid of the unvarnished cedar box. Back then, only the cigars in the colourful hinged lid boxes wore rings. Today, all Cuban cigars carry at least one ring, often more. And outside Cuba, bands tend to be even less restrained, increasingly colourful (or gaudy, depending on your view) and ever larger; the industry seems to be on a mission to cover the entire length of the cigar with a number of bands, until it resembles a polychromatic barber's pole. Some are brightly coloured, denoting the marque; others carry such useful information as the date of manufacture, the name of the cigar, the market for which it was made, the blend, the vintage, or indeed anything else that will provide an excuse to wind another little ring of paper around the glossy wrapper.

There is a theory that the cigar band was developed to stop gentlemen staining their gloves with the oils from the tobacco leaf. However, the accepted version is that it was a publicity stunt devised in 1850 by a German cigar merchant called Gustavo Bock who wanted to distinguish his cigars from others.

By the early twentieth century, whether you were an emperor, a king or a mere plutocrat, the personalised band was *le dernier cri*. Typically in Britain, a reaction against the trend decreed that it was infra dig in the extreme to leave the band on a cigar; however, in the last twenty years this has ceased to be of such importance, although the removal of bands is once more becoming a live issue as they cover ever more of the

cigar and need to be removed to actually smoke it. There is a risk that some of the glue that fastens the band to itself might become attached to the cigar, and that in removing the band, the wrapper will tear. The simple solution to this is to light the cigar and then, after a few minutes, once it has warmed up the glue, remove the band.

BLACK SHANK

A disease that rots the stalk of the tobacco plant, caused by the fungus *Phytophthora parasitica var. nicotianae*. Infection begins in the roots, often turning them as black as the rotted stem of the plant. It is easily spread by infected soil brought by machinery or the feet of workers and animals; and by excess water running off infected plants.

BLOOM

To the neophyte it looks unappealing, alarming even; however, to the aficionado this white deposit on the wrapper of an old cigar is a welcome sign that it has been aged correctly. It can be easily removed. British cigar expert Simon Chase has been known to keep a small brush about his person for this purpose, but I find that brief application of the silk Charvet *pochette* pulled from my outbreast pocket does the job equally effectively.

BLUE MOULD

Peronospora hyoscyami is a fungus that attacks tobacco plants during unusually wet, cold weather. It does not strike often, but when it takes hold the results can be devastating.

There was an outbreak of blue mould in Cuba in 1957, after which it disappeared for over 20 years. Then in 1979/1980 the disease wiped out almost all of Cuba's tobacco crop – Espino Morrero, a former director of Cuba's Tobacco Research Institute, puts the loss at 95 per cent. It returned to add to the country's woes during the early 1990s when Cuba was reeling after the surprise collapse of communism. There have also been serious outbreaks in Honduras and the Dominican Republic.

BN

Boite nature, a stouter, more upmarket take on the hinged-lid box; in plain cedar rather than plastered with colourful paper, with a clasp fastening and mitred corners and an inner lip or 'collar'. The most elaborate ones approach humidor levels of finish.

Box-pressed cigars have straight sides and a square or rectangular cross-section. Originally this was a result of cigars being packed in a box that was slightly too small for them, the effect accentuated when the boxes were stacked on top of each other for shipping and storage. Today it is an increasingly popular and desirable final shape – for example, Davidoff's box-pressed Nicaraguan. These cigars are shaped by ruler-like wooden slats being placed between them; after pressure has been applied, the cigars are turned and the process is repeated, in effect using a straight-sided mould to finish them. This is known as trunk-pressing and delivers more angular sides than box-pressing, which tends to retain some slight curvature.

Davidoff Nicaraguan box-pressed Toros

BROADLEAF

A thick and, as the name suggests, broad-leafed tobacco; not the most refined of plants.

Rather than individual leaves being harvested and hung in the curing barn, the plant is hacked down as if it were a small tree and hung in its entirety.

BUNCHING

There is much debate about the way in which the filler leaves are prepared and packed into the body of the cigar. *Entubado* refers to the technique of rolling them into tubes and then bunching them together.

This is generally accepted as the most effective method. The aim is to ensure the best draw, and if performed by an expert roller, such as the fabled Hamlet – whom I serendipitously met when he worked at Havana's Romeo y Julieta factory, and who is now something of a rock-star roller with Rocky Patel – *entubado* will demonstrate spectacular results, with an even draw throughout the cigar. However, it is hard to perfect and demands more skill than the rival school of rolling, the accordion method, in which the leaves are pleated like a paper fan.

This method tends to be quicker, and while not as highly regarded by connoisseurs, it is more dependable in the hands of less talented rollers.

A third and inferior style of rolling is the book method, which as the name suggests, involves layering the filler leaves one on top of another and then folding the sides inwards like the pages of a book.

CABINET SELECTION

At the beginning of the twentieth century, large consignments of cigars were stored in elaborately finished cabinets, often the size of wardrobes or sideboards, each holding thousands of cigars, which were packed in bundles of 50 or 25 into boxes with sliding lids.

CAPA

Not to be confused with the cap of leaf that crowns the head of cigar, capa is the Spanish term for 'wrapper'.

CAPOTE

Not to be confused with the American author, or the Cuban artist, *capote* is the Spanish term for 'filler'.

L
E
X
I
C
O
N

CHAVETA

The flat semicircular blade used by cigar rollers.

CHURCHILL

The most famous cigar smoker ever to apply a match to the end of a tube of Vuelta Abajo tobacco, Britain's wartime leader kept up such a ferocious consumption of cigars that at the end of the war he was described by Lord Halifax, ambassador to the United States, as the cigar manufacturers' best customer in the Empire. Halifax said that the Prime Minister smoked three cigars each hour during the 18 hours a day that he was awake. 'What he doesn't smoke he eats,'[1] he added. Fifty-four cigars a day is some going, even for Churchill. But it must be noted that the two men had been rivals for the Prime Minister's job when Chamberlain had resigned,

[1]   'Halifax on the Churchill cigar', *New York Times*, 13 May 1945

and Halifax had advocated coming to terms with Nazi Germany in 1940, so perhaps he was not the most reliable or charitable commentator on Winston's tobacco intake.

Nevertheless his observations indicate the totemic power of Churchill's cigars. During the war, boxes of cigars donated by the Prime Minister had been among the most sought-after lots auctioned for the war effort, with one raising the then staggering sum of '$211 apiece'[2] (a total of $2,110 for a box of ten) to aid Russian relief when sold at Christie's in 1943.

Certainly Havana was not slow in realising the marketing potential of the British premier, and he was rapidly adopted as a mascot by the cigar industry. 'Cuban Town Honors Churchill' ran the headline in the *New York Times* on 7 November 1942. 'The Provincial Council of Pinar del Río Province voted today to make Winston Churchill an honorary citizen. The resolution pronounced the British Prime Minister "an eminent son" of Vuelto Abajo,

[2] 'Churchill's cigars', *New York Times*, 17 October 1943

the region that grows the tobacco used in his famous cigars.'[3] Ironically, it took the City of London until the following year to bestow a similar honour.

His heroic contribution to cigar smoking is of course celebrated with an eponymous cigar, the Churchill, which before he took it on had been named the Clemenceau, after the cigar-loving French politician who led France to victory in the Great War and hosted the peace negotiations. But by the 1950s, 'brand' Churchill was clearly stronger than 'brand' Clemenceau, and following his visit to Cuba in February 1946, Romeo y Julieta launched the Churchill. However the size was still sometimes referred to as the Clemenceau until the 1980s.

Intriguingly an excellent little book called *Churchill's Cigar* dates the appearance of the first Churchill-banded cigar back to 1941, when New Yorker Sam Kaplan asked Lord Halifax to get a box of Havanas to Churchill that had been made especially for him and which carried his name. As regards the Romeo y Julieta story, the book's author, Stephen McGinty, has some doubt about whether Churchill even visited the factory during his trip to the island the year after the war.

> *Although there is some evidence that he paid a visit to the Romeo y Julieta factory, it is far from convincing. There is no listing or mention in contemporary press reports, yet there is a surviving eyewitness who insisted it took place. Jorge was a young roller of fourteen when, as he asserts, Churchill visited the plant. As Jorge rolled*

---

[3] 'Cuban Town Honors Churchill', *New York Times*, 7 November 1942

A selection of today's Romeo y Julieta Churchills

the longest cigars (those favoured by Winston) he was introduced to him, along with a group of other rollers. 'I could see him, but I was not so close.' A second point to support his recollection is that, following the visit, Romeo y Julieta became the first cigar company to brand this large cigar as 'Churchill's'.

However, 'Doubts over whether Churchill's visit to the factory ever took place grow when it is considered that there are no pictures of what would have been a considerable publicity coup. Perhaps Churchill forbade it, we do not know.'

When it comes to cigars and Churchill, fact and fiction are not always easy to separate. One particularly tall tale, alas apocryphal, is the claim by Gregorio Fuentes – 'the Cuban fisherman who, as captain of the *Pilar*, Ernest Hemingway's boat, became the inspiration for *The Old Man and the Sea* – to have hosted a cigar-smoking competition between Churchill and Hemingway'.[4] This is surely one of the greatest sporting

[4] Stephen McGinty, *Churchill's Cigar* (Macmillan, 2014), pp.138–9

CHURCHILL

contests that never was, but apparently Hemingway was not even in Cuba when Churchill visited in 1946.

According to McGinty, for many years Churchill was sent cigars by a Cuban brewer called Giraudier, who had befriended the former Prime Minister on his 1946 visit and allowed him the use of his private beach.

> *He began by sending, three times each year, a batch of 500 'Larrañaga' cigars, which Churchill had told him were unavailable in Britain. A cheque for £60 followed via the British Legation to cover duty charges. The ten packs of fifty cigars would arrive with the seasons in October, January and April, and when asked if the vitola was to his taste, Churchill replied: 'You wish to know if I like this brand. I do not think they could be bettered.' He thanked Giraudier for paying the duty, explaining that while he had the finances, he was unable to access the dollars due to restrictions in the currency exchange. He signed off: 'I wish I could spend a week of bathing on your beautiful beach.'*[5]

And while the regime change at the end of the 1950s did not favour businessmen such as Giraudier, Fidel Castro wanted to keep up the tradition and sent Sir Winston a box of cigars. To Churchill's chagrin, the British ambassador said it could not be accepted on account of Castro being a revolutionary with 'blood on his hands'.[6]

Even in the early twenty-first century, having made

[5]   Ibid., p.145

[6]   Ibid., p.163

cigars for Sir Winston was still a proud boast. During the early years of the century I met a sun-wizened septuagenarian called Rodolfo Leiva. Hot Rod, as he was known to his friends, was an infant prodigy who started rolling cigars at the age of 11, long before the revolution. He told me that at 15 years old he had rolled cigars for Sir Winston.

By the time I met him, his speciality was the *peludo*, or 'shaggy', a long Torpedo with an uncut end, for which he had gained quite a fan base. Sold unbanded, these cigars became legendary. Although it was generally illegal for US citizens to visit Cuba in those days, it was not unknown for American plutocrats to sail in on their yachts to visit Hot Rod and stock up on shaggies. Churchill would have approved, just as his family approved the use of the Winston Churchill name by Davidoff for a range of cigars using tobacco from Nicaragua, Mexico, Ecuador and the Dominican Republic.

CIBAO VALLEY

The tobacco-growing lands of the Dominican Republic.

COLOUR

One of my favourite things when visiting a cigar factory is seeing the *escogedores* (colour graders) at work. There are five principal colour groups, ranging from the pale caramel of Claro, via Colorado Claro, Colorado and Colorado Maduro to the almost black Oscuro. Within these five groups there are at least 60 recognised shades.

Wrapper-leaf colours, like so much else in life, are subject to fashion. In America during the 1950s and 1960s there was a trend for Candela wrappers, which were very pale and had a green tint to them that was achieved by careful heating in the curing barn to fix the chlorophyll.

By contrast today there is a marked trend to Maduro wrappers, which have a less glossy and elegant appearance. But visual appeal aside, dark Maduro wrappers make a definite contribution to the taste, imparting a sweetness or eucalyptus-like flavour. My personal inclination is towards Claro or Colorado Claro, with the sheen of the tobacco leaves' natural oils.

CONDEGA

Along with Jalapa and Estelí, one of the three most prominent growing regions of Nicaragua.

CUBA

The *locus classicus* of the cigar, occupying the same cultural position that France does among wine-making countries, Cuba remains the producing nation against which all others are judged; which is not the same as saying that all the cigars it makes are *ipso facto* better than those of other countries.

That said, the sheer variety of flavours and aromas that can be coaxed from Cuban leaf means that if I only had Cuban cigars to enjoy for the rest of what I hope will be a long life, I would not have too much to complain about.

CUTTER

Almost everyone has their own way of cutting a cigar, but Edward Sahakian of Davidoff of London has the best advice, given to him by Zino Davidoff himself: 'Zino used to tell me that if properly cut, the area of tobacco exposed at the head of the cigar should be the same or almost the same as the open end at the foot.'[7]

Of course such advice only works on a *Parejo* (straight-sided cigar). Each *Figurado* (shaped or pointed cigar) will differ, but around 4 mm from the point is a good place to start. With all cigars, try not to cut below the cap otherwise the wrapper will unravel.

Increasing ring gauges require ever-sharper guillotines with ever-bigger apertures, and the arrival of supersize cigars has led to the popularity of double-bladed guillotines that slice through the tobacco more readily and deliver a

[7]   Edward Sahakian, interview with the author, April 2016

L
E
X
I
C
O
N

CUTTER

more even cut. The trouble with using the traditional single-blade guillotine on a larger ring gauge is that if there is the slightest hint of dullness, the blade will crush and mangle rather than cut (impairing enjoyment and in very extreme cases destroying the cigar, damaging the wrapper, crushing airways and so on).

So-called 'V' cutters that take a notch out of the end of the cigar were considered out of date until Xikar released a new-style one, sparking a mini revival. The advantage claimed for the V cut is that it is unlikely to remove the cap of the cigar, whereas the wrapper of an injudiciously guillotined cigar can, as previously mentioned, unravel.

Needle-like cigar piercers are perfectly all right to collect and admire as antiques but are generally held to be irrelevant in today's cigarscape.

DATE CODES

Since 1985, boxes of Havana cigars have been stamped with the date of manufacture. On boxes made during the twenty-first century, the code has been simple: three-letter abbreviations of the month in Spanish:

ENE	FEB	MAR
Enero/January	Febrero/February	Marzo/March
ABR	MAY	JUN
Abril/April	Mayo/May	Junio/June
JUL	AGO	SEP
Julio/July	Agosto/August	Septiembre/September
OCT	NOV	DIC
Octubre/October	Noviembre/November	Diciembre/December

These three letters are followed by two digits identifying the year; 'ENE 17', for example, indicates that the box in question was manufactured in January 2017.

However, before the twenty-first century, the date of manufacture of a box of cigars appeared to be regarded as a low-to-mid-level state secret and was indicated in code on the bottom of the box. Initially it was a simple substitution of the letters NIVELACUSO for the numbers 1234567890 ('nivel acuso' is an obscure shipping term roughly meaning 'changing level' so chosen because it has 10 letters). Thus a box stamped USA (897) indicates a date of August 1997, while NOUL (1085) indicates a date of October 1985.

At first I do not remember people being that interested in this code, but when the cigar boom of the mid-1990s took off, people thought themselves frightfully clever for being able to turn a box over and confidently read off the date of manufacture. However, these amateur cryptographers were in for a shock from 1998, when a new code word, CODIGUNETA, was introduced and the numbers were switched around too, to 9876501234; thus a box made in January 1999 would be stamped UNCC.

Of course, cigar lovers of a Bletchley Park disposition, among them London cigar merchant and auctioneer Mitchell Orchant, soon cracked it, and in May 1999, the Cuban cigar industry fired up its Enigma machine and came up with a new system. From May to December 1999 the date codes were:

EP00	*ES00*	*EU00*	*EA00*
May	June	July	August
E000	*LE00*	*LL00*	*LR00*
September	October	November	December

And then, having played codemaker to the cigar smoker's codebreaker, the Cuban cigar industry did one of those predictably unpredictable things that make the world of the Havana cigar so engrossing and dispensed with codes altogether, simply marking each box with the abbreviations of month and year that has simplified the business of laying down boxes for ageing.

EDICIÓN LIMITADA

[*See*: *LIMITED EDITIONS*, page 94]

EDICIÓN REGIONAL

[*See*: *REGIONAL EDITIONS*, page 109]

ENTUBADO

[*See*: *BUNCHING*, page 74]

FACTORY CODES

As the Cuban economy is centralised and all the brands are the property of the state, no one factory produces a single marque. So while a cigar may have a home – Cohiba at El Laguito and so on – production for additional cigars is assigned to factories with spare capacity.

The Romeo y Julieta factory, now the home of the H. Upmann factory

The manufacturing process of Havana cigars is labyrinthine, and I suppose that in the spirit of a socialist centralised economy in which all factories were created equal, it makes no difference which factories manufacture which cigars. Instead production is distributed across the factories in Havana and beyond, with the blend being centrally determined and supplied. However, in practice some factories have proved more equal than others and, especially during the cigar boom of the 1990s, seasoned smokers scrutinised the base of boxes for the letters denoting the name of the factory.

FACTORY CODES

Although the factories are known colloquially by their pre-revolutionary names (Partagás, El Rey del Mundo, etc.), the letters stamped on the boxes often refer to the heroes of the revolution after whom they were renamed following the ousting of Batista.

After the revolution, the Romeo y Julieta factory was named Briones Montoto (BM); Partagás was christened Francisco Pérez Germán (FPG); the Heroes of Moncada (HM) had José Piedra named in their honour; El Rey del Mundo became Carlos Balino (CB); Miguel Fernández Roig (FR) gave his name to La Corona; and José Martí (JM), the arch Cuban patriot, had his name assigned to the old H. Upmann factory.

This information was rapidly decoded by cigar lovers, who identified certain star factories and eschewed others. This approach was particularly relevant during the late 1990s, when demand soared and production in Cuba, beset with shortages and difficulties, was uneven. In order to discourage this tendency, between 1998 and 2003 factory codes were changed three times.

The current system, in place since 2003, is widely described as largely unbreakable, with each factory assigned a three-letter code that can be changed as frequently as once a month, creating a level of encryption that has so far frustrated any effort at wholesale decoding. Moreover, since demand has eased and quality improved, factory identification has proved less necessary than before.

FIGURADO

[*See: TORPEDO*, page 147]

HABANOS S.A.

The Havana-based commercial entity that distributes Cuban cigars worldwide.

HUNTERS & FRANKAU

When I first got to know Hunters & Frankau, the UK importer of Havana cigars, the company was just 200 years old, and Nick Freeman was chairman. Now his daughter Jemma runs the firm and in 2015 it celebrated its 225th anniversary with the Ramón Allones Hunters & Frankau Aniversario 225. This 50 ring gauge, 5½ in/140 mm *cabeza tumbada* (dropped-head, or sloping-shouldered cigar that lacks the defined point of a Pirámide) references just one of the fascinating episodes in the firm's history, when between 1911 and 1927, as John Hunter, Morris & Elkan Ltd, it owned Ramón Allones, which made a similar-looking cigar called the Petit Nacional.

At around the time that Hunters sold Ramon Allónes (to Alonso Menendez), the rival firm of Frankau, owned by D. G. Freeman, Jemma's great-grandfather, acquired H. Upmann. By the end of the war, the Freeman family controlled one of the largest cigar businesses in what was still the British Empire, and in 1947 it was bought by Gallaher.

There the story might have ended had not Robert Freeman, known as 'The Colonel', decided to leave the board of Gallaher in 1952 and buy back the name of J. Frankau, to which he added the venerable firm of Hunters. Once restrictions on the importation of Cuban cigars were lifted in 1953, the company specialised in the importation and distribution of fine Havanas, a tradition that has continued to this day.

KELNER TASTING SYSTEM

Davidoff's Hendrik 'Henke' Kelner has consecrated his life to analysing and understanding tobacco, and this enlightenment has resulted in the concept of total palate stimulation that is today the Davidoff leitmotif. The way Henke demonstrates this is to make three cigars – except technically they are not cigars; rather cylinders of tobacco – out of the three classic tobaccos cultivated in the Dominican Republic – Olor, San Vicente and Piloto Cubano – and then offer them to his audience to smoke one at a time.

The first is the Olor, which stimulates the front of the tongue with sweet and then salty flavours. Next is the San Vicente; this, says Henke, is the equivalent of the lemon juice we might add to simple grilled fish and is sensed at the side of the tongue, stimulating saliva. The Piloto Cubano delivers what Kelner refers to as a linear flavour that goes from the front to the back of the tongue, a characteristic of Cuban cigars. Finally he presents his audience with a cigar made from all three of the tobaccos that they have tasted separately, to see how they combine to illustrate his goal of total palate stimulation.

'Our philosophy, is that the cigar is a friend. And what do you expect from a good friend?' he asks rhetorically. 'To be loyal, balanced, and a pleasure to spend time with. This is a good friend. What you appreciate most in a friend is a consistent friend, always the same friend, no surprises. This is just as important with a cigar. You need to build a relationship with cigars, and every day, every week, every month, every year, you need to maintain the same type of stimulation, for a consistent cigar is a consistent friend.'[8] Anyone, he says, can make a good cigar; the difficult thing is to make a consistently good cigar, and it begins with the leaf.

The way he describes it, cigar making is a cross between assembling a jigsaw puzzle, and a kaleidoscope in which the pieces are constantly changing: seed, soil, climate and position of the leaf on the plant are just four of the key variables.

When you combine the soil with a seed, that gives the typical type of stimulation. A particular seed in a particular soil has the genetic capacity to assimilate different nutrients, in different proportions, given the composition of the soil. The level and strength of that assimilation depends on the position of the leaf on the plant, and of course the weather. In the dry season the flavour is stronger. But in the rainy season, when you have less sun and more water, you have less photosynthesis, and more dilution of the nutrients when they are assimilated by the plant. Factor number five, the agricultural practice, can modify everything. For this reason we try to maintain the same type of agricultural practice; for example, how mazny plants per acre you're planting. If you're planting more, you will have smaller plants with the same nutrients.[9]

To listen to Henke for any length of time is to have the mind opened to the near-limitless flavour possibilities and combinations that can be conjured from the tobacco leaf.

....

[8]   Henrik Kelner, interview with the author, June 2016

[9]   Ibid.

EDIFICIO DE LA FABRICA DE TABACOS "LA CORONA"

LA CORONA FACTORY

The old factory dated from the turn of the century and was reputedly the first metal-framed building to be built in Havana. I have a fondness for it because it was where, in the mid-1990s, I met Taboada, a legendary roller who used to make bundles of 50 Salomones that were among the finest cigars I ever enjoyed.

Alas the factory closed some years ago and Taboada is no longer among the living. Today La Corona is housed in a mid-twentieth-century building in Havana's Vedado district.

LEAF

Until a few years ago I was only aware of three classifications of filler leaf. In ascending order of strength these are: *volado*, from the bottom, for combustibility; *seco*, from the middle, for aroma and some of the flavour; and further up the plant, the slower-burning *ligero*, which imparts strength and accounts for the steeple of ash that forms at the end of a lit cigar after the first ash has fallen.

Then, when the Cohiba Behike appeared, the world discovered (or rediscovered) a fourth leaf, *medio tiempo*, which comes from the very top of the sun-grown tobacco plant and was once used only in cigars destined for domestic consumption. But tastes have changed and what was once regarded as too powerful for export is, when properly treated and expertly blended, like the seasoning that raises a dish from tasty to exquisite. There are just two *medio tiempo* leaves per plant and they cannot be relied upon to appear every year. It is this secret ingredient that accounts for the rich, nuanced and surprisingly subtle flavour of the Cohiba Behike.

LEAF CLASSIFICATIONS

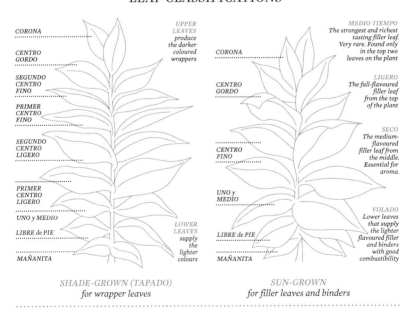

CORONA

CENTRO GORDO

SEGUNDO CENTRO FINO

PRIMER CENTRO FINO

SEGUNDO CENTRO LIGERO

PRIMER CENTRO LIGERO

UNO y MEDIO

LIBRE de PIE

MAÑANITA

UPPER LEAVES produce the darker coloured wrappers

LOWER LEAVES supply the lighter colours

SHADE-GROWN (TAPADO)
for wrapper leaves

CORONA

CENTRO GORDO

CENTRO FINO

UNO y MEDIO

LIBRE de PIE

MAÑANITA

MEDIO TIEMPO
The strongest and richest tasting filler leaf. Very rare. Found only in the top two leaves on the plant

LIGERO
The full-flavoured filler leaf from the top of the plant

SECO
The medium-flavoured filler leaf from the middle. Essential for aroma.

VOLADO
Lower leaves that supply the lighter flavoured filler and binders with good combustibility

SUN-GROWN
for filler leaves and binders

Meanwhile outside Cuba, the more experimental farmers and makers have added a further classification, *visos*, that describes the four leaves between *seco* and *ligero*, the logic being that on a 16-leaf plant, the difference in flavour between the fifth and twelfth leaves is too great to be described by one category.

LIGADOR

Master blender.

LIGERO

[*See*: *LEAF*, page 92]

LIMITED EDITIONS

The twenty-first-century obsession with exclusivity is a marketing man's dream: to feel unique and special is the goal, and the limited edition is one of the tools for achieving it. Thus the cigars known in Havana as Edición Limitada have become an eagerly anticipated annual event. Of course, Cuba being Cuba, part of the entertainment resides in seeing whether the cigars actually arrive in the market within the year stated on their band. Edición Limitada cigars are characterised by dark, almost Maduro-coloured wrappers. The idea is to present a familiar brand in an unfamiliar *vitola* (size and shape) currently not in the brand line-up.

Since the programme's introduction in 2000, limited editions have become incredibly popular and have accounted for some truly outstanding cigars, including the best cigar of

the century thus far, the Cohiba Sublime [*above*]. However, as Simon Chase, British cigar expert and director of Havana cigar importers Hunters & Frankau explains, had it not been for a scarcity of wrappers for larger cigars at the beginning of the century, Havanaphiles would have been denied this annual excitement. Happily, necessity took on its traditional role as the parent of ingenuity, and the rest, as they say, was fragrant blue smoke and silvery ash.

'They were looking at anything,' recalls Chase, 'and discovered a load of leaf for wrappers taken from the top of the plant for domestic production. When I arrived in June of 2000 they showed me a box of these dark-wrapped creatures. They were having this huge debate as to whether they would release them and I explained that there are a lot of people who like a dark cigar in a richer blend.'[10]

At first the limited edition programme was agreeably haphazard. The debut batch appeared in November 2000, and their black and gold band only carried the words Edición Limitada, without any indication of a year. The limited edition cigars of 2001 did carry the year on their band but did not appear until halfway through 2002.

....
[10] Simon Chase, interview with the author, April 2016

L
E
X
I
C
O
N

Thereafter things settled down, as much as they can where Cuba is concerned, and after an uncertain start the cigars are now a cherished part of the cigar calendar. Particularly popular editions, such as H. Upmann Magnum 50 and Cohiba Pirámides, have been known to enter standard production at a later date.

At their launch, it was announced that Edición Limitada cigars would be clothed in wrappers that were a minimum of two years old, and in 2007 this age threshold was extended to cover all tobacco in the cigar.

[*See: APPENDIX A*, page 229,
for a detailed list of limited editions]

MATURATION

Ageing is one of the most fascinating and least understood aspects of the cigar. A cigar is more than just a smoke, as Kipling would have us believe; it is an ongoing biochemical process. As a natural product, it is changing all the time, and these changes can be exacerbated by external environmental

Davidoff Chateau Yquem

factors: heat, cold, moisture, dryness, etc. It is constantly altering in character, taste and strength, and it is this mutability that makes cigars so absorbing.

Recent years have seen cigars being released and smoked too young (at least in my opinion); this in turn has shaped tastes among some cigar smokers for the harsher, less harmonious flavours of youth. The telltale whiff of ammonia from a freshly opened box of cigars is a sure indicator that more time is required, and that if cut and lit the flavours are likely to be astringent and unbalanced – but if that is what your palate is used to, then that might be exactly what you are after. I regard it as infanticide.

For the real cigar snob there is nothing like an aged Havana cigar, preferably a Davidoff from the 1980s, or a Dunhill Cabinetta, a desirability reflected in the fact that prices for these and other rare cigars are only getting higher. Many vintage Davidoffs still taste exquisite, and continue to develop. Some aficionados swear that many pre-revolutionary cigars still show signs of life and can be enjoyed;

Dunhill Don Candido 506

MATURATION

in my limited experience, that pulse is sometimes faint and vital signs are hard to detect, as much of the flavour and strength has departed over the decades. However, if the cigar was good to begin with and has been impeccably maintained over generations (two very big ifs), the results can be stunning. Think of it like chasing ghosts of flavours across your palate and savouring aromas of a rare refinement and delicacy.

Anything dating back to before the 1940s will give an insight into the style of cigars before even the Criollo and Corojo were introduced. But the flavour and aroma are so time-tempered as to be fragile and evanescent, and of course there is a psychological effect to be considered. One respected cigar collector explained to me how he had observed that when he handed an old or rare cigar to friends, they held and smoked it differently. These are mainly bought by collectors who feel that they are acquiring a piece of history, who find the quality of the design and lithography appealing and who appreciate the exquisite care and ingenuity with which these cigars were packaged, but who aren't necessarily planning to set fire to them.

The concept of ageing cigars is not a new one but it is gaining in popularity. Obviously, given that cigars are an agricultural product with many of the same attendant snobberies and gastronomic pretensions, it is natural to draw parallels with the ageing of fine wine. The primary function of laying down wine was, at first, to make it drinkable. As vinification techniques improved, ageing in the bottle was not an absolute necessity but nonetheless improved the contents.

I no longer drink, but from what I can recall, the ageing of wine is a fairly well-documented business: after a certain number of years the wine reaches a peak from which it gradually descends. In my experience, the ageing of cigars is not quite so predictable. Instead of progressing through an arc, it reminds me more of the pattern of waves moving across the screen of an oscilloscope, and where one catches the cigar on its undulating journey through time has a profound effect on the flavour and strength.

Sometimes a cigar when first tasted comes across as docile and mild, only to present completely differently a few years later. That happened to me with a batch of cigars rolled for the twenty-fifth anniversary of the Davidoff shop in London in 2005, which were initially mild with a crisp edge. I came across one six years later and lit it to discover a completely different cigar altogether, lively to the point of being almost combative.

Ageing of leaf is completely different to ageing in the box, and there are plenty of opportunities to taste mature leaves rolled into cigars. Since 2007, Edición Limitadas [*see*: *LIMITED EDITIONS*, page 94] have been made with tobacco that has been aged in bales for a minimum of two years. Reservas, launched in Cuba in 2003, are made with tobacco that has been aged in bales for a minimum of three years. Grand Reservas, which first appeared in 2009, are made with tobacco with a minimum of five years' bale age.

And of course boxes are date-stamped, giving a vintage of sorts. However, this is not to be confused with the vintage that appears on a bottle of wine. The latter indicates the year in which the grapes in a certain vineyard were harvested, while by its nature a cigar is a skilful blend of different tobaccos from different farms, different districts and, in the case of many non-Havanas, different countries, which fulfil different purposes and take different lengths of time to reach their usefulness, making it harder to assign a vintage to a box of cigars in the way in which winemakers do.

However, the year and even the month in which the cigars are made can give vital clues if one has the knowledge [*see*: *DATE CODES*, page 84 and *STAMPS, SEALS & STICKERS*, page 137]. For instance, at around the turn of the century, wrappers on Cuban cigars were especially fine and delicate, with a tendency towards unravelling or splitting once the cigar was cut; this could be due to the use at the time of the Habano 2000 seed, which while high-yielding produced thinner wrappers.

Moreover, given that the quality and abundance of tobacco changes from year to year, blends that are intended to remain identical and true to the expectation of the smoker can never be entirely consistent. However, the maintenance of a large and carefully documented inventory of tobacco built up over many years, such as that held at Davidoff's facilities in the Dominican Republic, gives the blender greater scope for creating consistent cigars.

Ageing begins as the cigar is being rolled. Upon arrival at the factory, the leaves are moistened to make them pliable, and although this is a gentle misting rather than a total drenching, they still retain some of the moisture that triggers a small fermentation – not as powerful as those undergone at the sorting and stripping houses, but enough to require the cigars to be rested in the dark and cool of the *escaparate*. The *escaparate* is to a cigar factory what a vault is to a bank. To walk as I have done many times around the *escaparates* of Havana's legendary factories, seeing the oily wrappers glinting jewel-like in the penumbral light and

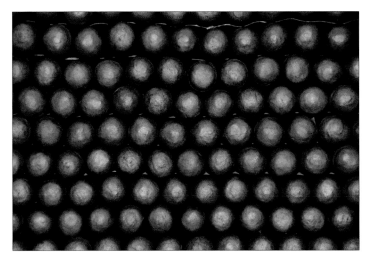

Cigars ageing in Davidoff's Dominican Republic escaparate

savouring the aroma that fills and thickens the air, is one of the great experiences that life has to offer. However, it is not always such a pleasure: at the height of the cigar boom, I recall visiting an *escaparate* in the Dominican Republic that smelt so chokingly strongly of ammonia that my eyes watered and I had to make my excuses and go outside to take some air.

Once the *escaparate* has worked its magic, the cigars are banded and boxed. It is at this time that they enter the 'sick' period (the name given to the time during which a cigar should not be smoked because the individual flavours of the tobacco are melding); there may even be lingering traces of ammonia, created by the final fermentation. Smoking a young and newly landed cigar can result in a mouthful of harsh, acidic, jagged and unformed flavour. Tasting it at this time is only of academic interest, as the experienced palate can usually detect whether the cigar has the potential and structure to age well; cigars during this period display the characteristics of tannin associated with young Bordeaux and the acidity of the *vins clairs* of Champagne. At this stage the best you can do with a box of young cigars is to leave it with your cigar merchant, or put it in your cellar, as the dark, dampish, ventilated conditions and relatively stable temperature will suit them.

This is not to say that fresh cigars cannot be smoked quite happily, especially in their birthplace. I have often smoked cigars straight from the roller's bench in Cuba and the Dominican Republic. The tropics are blessed with a climate and humidity that makes them ideal not just for cultivating tobacco but for storing the finished product. Cuba is like one giant humidor; cigars can be left in the open without fear of them drying out, and the free circulation of air along with the heat can be counted upon to get rid of disagreeable ammonia smells.

After time, the nicotine level will decrease and the harsher, more bitter flavours abate. However, it is often these

Ramon Allónes Coronas de Lujo

bitter, tannic tastes that indicate the structure of the cigar; regard them as the skeleton on which the other flavours hang. Let them dissipate too much and the character of the cigar will begin to fade away. As always, the right time to enjoy an aged cigar (provided it has been looked after properly throughout its journey to maturity) is a matter of personal taste.

There are many variables beyond environmental conditions that influence ageing. The format of the cigar is an obvious one: the larger the cigar, the longer it takes for the various tobaccos to interact and the chemical processes to weld their different characters into one harmonious whole (similar to the way in which wine matures more slowly in magnums than in 75cl bottles). Size also brings into play the difference in proportion between wrapper and filler. Packaging too plays its part: the contents of a hinged-lid box matures more rapidly than a cabinet bundle of 25, which in turn matures more rapidly than a half-wheel of 50 cigars, while tubes or ceramic and glass jars mature entirely differently as they tend to be airtight.

As a rule of thumb so vague that it is really more of a subjective and empirical hunch, a mild cigar such as an H. Upmann or a Rey del Mundo will benefit from up to five years of ageing; a medium-strength cigar such as a Romeo or a Montecristo will benefit from up to 10 years of ageing; and the larger, more complex and fuller-flavoured cigars such as Bolívar, and particularly Partagás, as well as Cohiba, can take over a decade to reach their full potential. But even a couple of years will yield tangible results.

After they have reached their peak, different cigars will behave in different often unexpected ways, which is where the oscilloscopic simile comes in. In general, stronger cigars with more pronounced characteristics have a good core of flavour and are sufficiently robust to warrant long-term ageing.

Oriental cigar author Min Ron Nee, whose *Illustrated Encyclopedia of Post-Revolution Havana Cigars* is essential if not particularly portable reading, has defined these stages further, calling them the second and third maturation periods, and has developed a scientific theory based on discussions with wine and whisky experts.

What Nee describes as the second maturation is, he says, 'the result of degradation of tannin and the interaction of its end products with the flavours generated by fermentation. All young cigars have a "tannic" taste, to a different degree. An excessive tannic taste is "dry" on the mouth, "green" and "harsh". It is believed to be, as its name suggests, the taste of tannin, a natural ingredient of plant structures. It can only be tasted by the tongue, as experiments have shown that the nose or the pharynx is incapable of "smelling" the tannic taste.'

His observations about the structure and behaviour of tannins are fascinating.

The chemical structure of tannin is long chained phenol polymers (in chemistry, a polymer is a long chain of similar organic molecules). They will break down with age into shorter chains or even single molecular phenol.

Of phenol molecules in plants, most are called non-aromatic phenol, the simplest form of phenol molecule. The burning of this type of phenol with oxygen results in the familiar 'tobacco taste', the aroma which you smell when burning a wood fire.

Some are called aromatic phenols, if the simple phenol ring has an attached organic side chain (the chemical structure of phenol is a hexagonal ring). When these aromatic phenol polymers break down into much shorter chains or even single molecules, they are believed to account for the taste of toasted tobacco. This is the most pleasant form of tobacco taste. As the name suggests, it smells of toasted bread.

As time goes by, when tannin breaks down into simpler molecules, these molecules react with other chemicals to form more organic molecules. As a result a lot of different pleasant flavours are generated in addition. **And it is at this point in the cigar's development that it may behave in a way that is 'uncharacteristic' of the blend as it is generally experienced in cigars that have yet to achieve great age** [author's bold] *(which the majority do not).*

The smooth aromatic woody flavours are believed to be aromatic simple polymers of aromatic phenols, or aromatic compounds generated by the chemical reaction of the simple polymers with other organic substances.

Of particular interest is the 'woody sweetness' (actually wood sugars) formed by degradation of tannin. These wood sugars continue to replenish the loss of sweetness generated by the fermentation process, and they have a different taste. [11]

[11]   Min Ron Nee, *An Illustrated Encyclopaedia of Post-Revolution Havana Cigars* (Interpro Business Corp, Hong Kong, 2003), pp 8–9

MEDIA RUEDA

Literally 'half-wheel' – a bundle of 50 cigars. Alas, in 2016 the Cuban cigar industry announced that it would no longer be selling cabinets of 50 cigars.

MEDIO TIEMPO

[*See*: *LEAF*, page 92]

MOULDS

Before the cigar is clothed in the wrapper, it is placed in a mould to ensure it is the correct shape. Originally cigars were rolled without moulds, a feat that needed to be accomplished with consistency, requiring strength and skill. Moulds were introduced from the second half of the nineteenth century.

Moulds in use during cigar rolling

PAREJO

A straight-sided cigar with a rounded head. All other shapes of cigars are known as Figurados [*q.v.,* page 147].

PARTAGÁS FACTORY

The parakeet-bright paintwork on the nineteenth-century facade of this building on a street behind the Capitol in Havana makes the world-famous Partagás factory unmistakable, as does the swarm of black-market vendors hovering in the street outside. Alas, it has not functioned as a working factory for a number of years. However, the shop and smoking room are a popular meeting point for overseas visitors.

Partagás factory

PLUME

A synonym for *BLOOM* [*q.v.,* page 72].

PROCIGAR

This association of cigar makers was founded in the Dominican Republic by Davidoff's Henke Kelner in 1992. The objectives of Procigar 'are to defend, protect and divulge the good name of the land of Cigar Country, number one exporter of Premium Cigars in the World'. Its aims are as much cultural as they are commercial: 'Preserving this heritage and maintaining the quality on which [it] is built – is the mission of the Association of Dominican Cigar Manufacturers, ensuring the Cigar Country's continued status as the world's number one premium cigar manufacturer.'[12]

The high point of the Procigar year is the festival that takes place in February, comprising factory visits, gala dinners and sundry other acts of merrymaking. In 2016, the membership stood at a dozen: General Cigar Dominicana, La Aurora, Quesada Cigars, Tabacalera de García, Tabadom Holdings (Davidoff), Tabaquisa, De Los Reyes Cigars, Tabacalera Fuente, Tabacalera La Alianza, La Flor Dominicana, Tabacalera Palma and PDR Cigars.

PURO

A *puro* is a cigar in which all tobacco – filler, binder and

---

[12] http://procigar.org/about-procigar, accessed 7 June 2016

wrapper – is the product of one country. The hand-made Havana cigars that are sold around the world are *puros*. However, production across much of the rest of the Caribbean and Central America has tended to be a mixture of tobaccos from different countries, giving blenders a broader palette of flavours to draw upon and allowing certain regions to specialise: for instance, Ecuador is known for its wrapper leaf. This is in part a legacy of the time when these nations were primarily exporters of leaf tobacco that was rolled into cigars in the USA and other countries.

REGIONAL EDITIONS

Regional editions, cigars made for one particular country or region, came into being in Havana in 2005. The criteria are a little complicated. The cigar must not be one of the internationally available brands; instead it has to be made in an unusual size in a brand chosen from a list of what are described as 'local' or 'multi-local' marques, some of which are famous – for instance Bolívar – others less so, such as Sancho Panza.

There were four regional editions in 2005 and six in 2006. It was the Por Larrañaga Magnifico, a subtle, floral, harmonious and aromatic cigar, released in Britain in 2007, that really captured the imagination of cigar smokers. Two years later, there were 23 regional editions.

As well as being a little-known brand in an unusual but desirable large size (50 × 6¾ in/170mm), the Magnifico established a pattern with its elaborate packaging. Regional editions tend towards what might be called cigar bling: as well as the regular band, they carry an extra paper ring

proclaiming their region. With the Magnifico [*above*], UK importers Hunters & Frankau went to extraordinary lengths to recreate the old Por Larrañaga band, using a specialist printer in Eindhoven with over a century of experience in printing for the cigar trade.

The following year saw another cult regional edition: the Phoenicios. Made for the Lebanese market in 2008, it adopted the then relatively new Sublimes format: a 54 ring gauge cigar around 6½ in/165mm in length. It is a highly regarded *vitola*; the best cigar so far of the twenty-first century is widely held to be the Cohiba Sublime, (a 2005 limited edition). Initial production was 6,000 boxes of 30 with a second run of 3,000 boxes of 15: scarce enough to stimulate interest, but nevertheless sufficiently available to create a market. Some, but by no means all, Regional Bolivians have risen in value.

Impressive on paper, the cigar is even better when one sets fire to it, as I had the pleasure of doing in 2015. The first half-inch is almost fresh and grassy, then it assumes the familiar pepperiness, but nuanced with herbaceous notes and a slight cedar undertone to keep the palate interested and to stop the cigar becoming monotonously overpowering. A second batch of Phoenicios was made to celebrate the thirtieth anniversary of the Middle Eastern distributor.

In 2015 another celebratory regional edition, the Ramón Allones Aniversario 225, was produced to mark the 225th anniversary of Hunters & Frankau [*see* page 89]. This cigar enjoyed extra ageing in the Hunters warehouse. While it has the underlying strength typical of a powerful Havanas, there is also subtlety and complexity, with hints of dark-roasted coffee beans and even a salted sweetness,

A selection from the bewildering variety of regional editions

all underpinned by a piquancy that augurs well for ageing. The packaging is spectacular even by the standards of regional editions, consisting of four sliding-lid boxes of 25 cigars stored inside a replica of the cabinets in which cigars were shipped to the UK in the early twentieth century.

But of course not all regional editions are of the same quality, and it is perhaps the proliferation of such editions that has caused Habanos, the marketing arm of the Cuban cigar industry, to tighten up the rules from 2016, permitting only one regional edition per territory per year and allowing the repetition of a brand only after five consecutive regional editions, each from different brands. In addition, the sizes and shapes will be limited.

[*See*: *APPENDIX B*, page 232,
for a detailed list of regional editions]

RELATIVE HUMIDITY

Simply put, relative humidity is a measure of the quantity of water vapour in the air relative to the maximum the air can hold before it reaches saturation point, when the moisture condenses and turns into rain.

Of course, relative humidity is anything but simple: the same amount of moisture can give different relative humidity readings. Relative humidity varies according to air temperature: the warmer it is, the more humidity the air can hold; correspondingly, the capacity for moisture retention in the air is lower when it is cooler. Along with different air composition, this contributes to the observation that cigars often taste different when smoked at sea level in the tropical heat and humidity of Cuba and the Dominican Republic rather than at several thousand metres above sea level in a ski resort in the middle of winter (although do not discount the power of the psychological effect of enjoying a cigar in the heart of cigar-making country or touring one of the great historical cigar factories).

If you like skiing and cigar smoking, choose to spend the winter in a resort such as Gstaad, which is not as high above sea level as St Moritz – snowfall may be less predictable, but in Gstaad (a little over 1,000 metres above sea level), cigars are still enjoyable.

RESERVA & GRAN RESERVA

During the 1999/2000 harvest in Cuba, it was decided to set aside select bales of tobacco leaves for an additional three years' maturation. The first of these Reserva cigars was a series of Cohibas in various sizes that was launched in 2003. They can still be found, but in my opinion they do not give the best idea of just how good these sensational Reservas can be.

After this trial run, the first 'real' Reserva was the Partagás Series D Reserva of 2005. As soon as I tasted it in the Partagás factory with the then director, I knew it was something special. I usually find Partagás a little on the powerful side, and this was certainly a full cigar, but there was a rich creaminess to it that really made the most of the Partagás characteristics; it was like a powerful Olympic medal-winning athlete clothed in an impeccably tailored suit from Terry Haste, Huntsman or Rubinacci.

To use a vinous rather than a sartorial analogy, I have also described a Reserva as being like a wine with extra barrel age. While the maturation of finished cigars (not unlike wine ageing in a bottle) allows them to settle, and the flavours of the different tobaccos to come together; the extra maturation of the raw material used for Reservas radically improves the tobacco with which the cigar is made. They are in effect made with much better tobacco; in a way this should be like (another abstruse simile coming up) watching the director's cut of a movie: a cigar that is the best it can be.

The best got better with the arrival of the Gran Reserva in 2009, made using tobacco leaves with a minimum of five years of age on them. The results can be sublime, as shown by the Partagás Lusitania Gran Reserva, which made its appearance in 2012. The Lusitania is Partagás's Double Corona, arguably its most famous *vitola*; a broom-stick of tobacco that tops seven and a half inches. This is an epic cigar, a triumph of the *torcedor*'s art, carrying within its succulent dark caramel-coloured wrapper all the rich complexity of a Partagás delivered with a refinement that is almost ethereal. Slightly smaller, and lighter in flavour, but almost as entrancing, is the Romeo y Julieta Churchill Reserva also released in 2012, made with tobacco from the 2008 harvest.

Partagás Gran Reserva 15 Lusitania

Of course, not all Reservas and Gran Reservas, all made with leaves harvested exclusively in the *vegas de primera* (top quality plantations) of the Vuelta Abajo, are as successful, and the idea is at its best when applied to brands with strength and character. For instance, the H. Upmann No.2 Reserva, made with tobacco from the 2010 harvest, while a very pleasant and pleasurable cigar indeed, failed – at least in my opinion – to scale the heights reached by the Partagás Reserva and Gran Reserva.

Consistency of manufacture is not perhaps always the strongest of the Cuban cigar industry's attributes; the quality of output varies from factory to factory. The most irritating problem is overfilling or poor de-stemming that leaves twigs inside a cigar, making it about as much pleasure to smoke as a pencil. Underfilling, which leads to a collapse in the side of the cigar, is far less irritating, but nonetheless disappointing. A batch of cigars hurried into production may assault the olfactory nerve with an ammoniac pungency. Or the problem may be purely aesthetic: the wrappers may be unduly harsh or spotted, for instance. Just as a restaurant prides itself on plating a dish with care and discrimination, so part of the pleasure of a cigar is beholding it before you set fire to it.

Such problems are highly unlikely with the Reserva and Gran Reservas. These cigars blur the line between craftsmanship and art; even the box is a thing of beauty, with its dark veneer and marquetry inlay.

If you can afford it, Reservas and Gran Reservas are what you should be smoking most of the time, but it takes more than mere money to lay your hands on them. They tend to be made in very, very small numbers. For instance, the worldwide supply of Gran Reserva Lusitanias was just 5,000 boxes of 15 cigars; and the Romeo y Julieta Reservas were barely more numerous; 5,000 boxes again, but this time with 20 cigars in a box.

It will be fascinating to see how the finished cigars mature with time (my hunch is that the best of them will improve for decades), but given that Reservas and Gran Reservas sell out almost as soon as they arrive, this is not a problem that most of us are likely to have to deal with.

RECENT RESERVAS

Cigar sizes are given as RING GAUGE × LENGTH

YEAR	BRAND	EDITION NAME	VITOLA	SIZE
2005	Partagás	Serie D No.4 Reserva Cosecha 2000	Robustos	50 × 4⅞ in/124 mm
2007	Montecristo	No.4 Reserva Cosecha 2002	Marevas	42 × 5⅛ in/130 mm
2012	Romeo y Julieta	Churchill Reserva Cosecha 2008	Julieta No.2	47 × 7 in/178 mm
2014	H. Upmann	No.2 Reserva Cosecha 2010	Pirámides	52 × 6⅛ in/155 mm
2016	Hoyo de Monterrey	Epicure No.2 Reserva Cosecha 2012	Robustos	50 × 4⅞ in/124 mm

RECENT GRAN RESERVAS

Cigar sizes are given as RING GAUGE × LENGTH

YEAR	BRAND	EDITION NAME	VITOLA	SIZE
2009	Cohiba	Siglo VI Gran Reserva Cosecha 2003	Canonazo	52 × 5⅞ in/150 mm
2011	Montecristo	No.2 Gran Reserva Cosecha 2005	Pirámides	52 × 6⅛ in/155 mm
2013	Partagás	Lusitanias Gran Reserva Cosecha 2007	Prominentes	49 × 7⅝ in/194 mm
2015	Romeo y Julieta	Wide Churchill Gran Reserva Cosecha 2009	Montesco	55 × 5⅛ in/130 mm

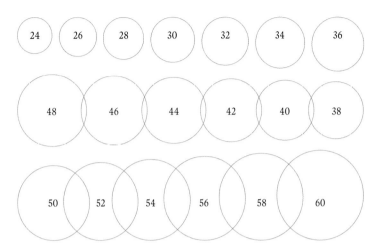

A measure of the diameter of a cigar; one ring gauge point is equivalent to $1/64$th of an inch. Over the course of the twenty-first century, the trend has been towards ever girthier cigars, with ring gauges of 60 not uncommon, and some exceeding that. They are on the whole inelegant, and risk dislocation of the jaw, but they do let the smoker and, far more importantly, the blender show off. It is no accident that *medio tiempo* made its appearance in the Cohiba Behikes with ring gauges from 52 to 56.

Bigger cigars can accommodate more leaves, and therefore heavier ring-gauge cigars are richer in flavour but cooler smoking than their slender counterparts, which concentrate their flavour on one part of the palate rather than filling the mouth and, if smoked too quickly or energetically, can heat up too rapidly, becoming harsh-tasting.

Thinner cigars are also a test of the blender, as the lower the ring gauge, the less easy it is to avoid blockages;

L
E
X
I
C
O
N

conversely, the heavier ring gauges can accommodate a little more in the way of debris blocking the airways, so a blockage that might ruin a 33 ring gauge Palma can be accommodated in a cigar with a ring gauge over 50. Of course in an ideal world no cigar would be plugged, but then in such a place we would have no corked bottles of wine, as well as world peace and goodwill to all men. That said, I cannot recall having to abandon a Davidoff because it was blocked, something to do, I daresay, with the fact that Davidoff is a Swiss company.

ROBUSTO

It is said that this size (50 × 4 in/102 mm) was first created for Leopold de Rothschild in the late nineteenth century (apparently it is still known by that name in parts of America), and like all things it has gone in and out of fashion ever since. There was a time in the 1980s when slim cigars were *le dernier cri* and the Robusto format was all but extinct. *Mirabile dictu*, in 1984 Cuba produced just 5,000 of its then most famous Robusto, the Partagás Serie D No. 4 For many years, the 50 ring gauge cigar (of which this is the classic example) was near the top end of the girth scale; now the Robusto is a standard cigar size offered by many brands. Classics include Romeo y Julieta's Short Churchill, Hoyo de Monterrey's Epicure No.2, Ramón Allones' Specially Selected, Bolívar's Royal Corona, Davidoff's Special R [*below*] and of course Cohiba's Robusto.

The José Manuel Seguí factory is located in a small county called Güira de Melena. This factory, and a few dozen more across the country, exists almost completely under the radar.

Although only 25 miles or so south of Havana, the ambience is entirely different. Güira de Melena is a place where horse and trap, bullock cart and bicycle are more commonly used than a car. By comparison Havana seems a cosmopolitan city of the future.

I first came to hear about the Seguí factory in 2007, when the Juan López Selección Suprema was launched in Britain. I had tasted some Juan López before and found them unmemorable; it was with low expectations that I clipped the end of this 52 × 6¹/₂ in/165 mm cigar. It was a revelation: smooth, flavoursome without being too strong, intensifying in strength incrementally rather than hitting the palate explosively. It was beautifully rolled; neither overfilled and hard to draw upon, nor with declivities indicating the underfilling that can lead to uneven burn. The wrapper was a marvel: silken, caramel in colour, with an inviting sheen.

I became curious to visit the factory where these had been made. I found a place of charming simplicity and Stakhanovite zeal. The director's office was a small room with nothing but a desk, paperless, computer free and without even a telephone. The *galera* where a hundred or so rollers worked was little more than a large barn. Floors were of stamped earth or corrugated metal. Air conditioning was unknown. Hospitality was warm and similarly rudimentary: a shot glass of rum with a splash of TuKola.

In general, no Havana factory produces a single marque. However, small runs of cigars such as limited editions or regional specialities, where production is in the tens rather than hundreds of thousands, often come from a single factory. When I first visited the Seguí factory, it was stacked with boxes of a limited edition from 2009; the H. Upmann Magnum 48, one of the best balanced of what I call 'espresso cigars', a 15-minute burst of flavour tailored to the needs of the cigar lover who has to contend with increasingly restrictive smoking laws.

Seguí turned out to have been responsible for some extremely desirable cigars: the Juan López Maximo, made for Switzerland in 2008; the Juan López Short Torpedo, which appeared the same year in the Caribbean; the Juan López Selección No.3 and No. 4, made for Belgium & Luxemburg and Asia respectively; and the Fonseca No. 4, also sold in the Low Countries. It is the rise of the regional edition that has brought the excellent work in the Seguí factory to the fore.

As with many of the best things in Cuba, it seems to have happened entirely by accident. When I interviewed him, the only explanation that the late Oscar Basulto, former co-president of Habanos SA, advanced for this rural centre of excellence was that 'as might happen everywhere, people from small towns seem to be more sensitive and hardworking than people from the city. A cigar factory in a small town is the heart of the village and so is highly appreciated by all the inhabitants who devote dedication and love to the factory in general.'

Originally from Iran, where his family was one of the nation's best known commercial dynasties, Edward Sahakian left Tehran for London at the end of the seventies. He did not think he would be gone long, so he travelled light: just his dinner jacket and a few kilos of caviar. Happily, his stay in England lasted longer than he envisaged, and since 1980 his Davidoff store on the corner of St James's and Jermyn Streets has been one of the great landmarks of the cigar world.

An expert in Cuban and non-Cuban cigars alike, Edward is everything a great cigar merchant should be: knowledgeable, discreet, stylish and excellent company; a legend in the cigar world, he is also far too modest to ever tell you as much. His experience of life and of cigars is unique. He is also a dear friend with whom it has been my pleasure to travel to both Havana and Santo Domingo and to play numerous games of backgammon. He has now been joined in the business by his son Eddie, and together they have opened a second venture: the Edward Sahakian Cigar Shop and Sampling Lounge at London's Bulgari Hotel. His company and his wisdom are both worth seeking out.

SAN JUAN y MARTINEZ

This small town in the Vuelta Abajo gives its name to a DOP (Denominación de Origen Protegida) and along with San Luis [*below*] is home to the finest *vegas de primera* in the Vuelta Abajo, including the historically significant Hoyo de Monterrey plantation. It is one of the two growing districts that supplies leaves for Cohiba.

SAN LUIS

This small town is to the Vuelta Abajo what Beaune is to Burgundy. It gives its name to a DOP and is home to famous plantations including El Corojo and Cuchillas de Barbacoa. Along with San Juan y Martinez, [*above*] it supplies leaves for Cohiba.

SBN

Semi boite nature – a hinged cedar-wood box with a clasp or stud fastening at the front. This is a less elegant and robust version of the BN (*boite nature*), and lacks the inner lip or collar. [*See also*: *SLB*, page 136 and *BN*, page 72].

SECO

[*See*: *LEAF*, page 92]

SEED

In Cuba in the mid-twentieth century, one of the most popular seed varieties was Pelo de Oro. Although strong, sweet and flavourful, it was susceptible to disease, especially blue mould. Today it is barely used and in its stead a range of hybrids has been developed.

For Cuba, the second half of the twentieth century was dominated by two varieties: Criollo and Corojo. Early in the century, the country had lost most of its native seeds, and it was only in the late 1920s that agronomist Juan Tomás Roig managed to reproduce the famous black Cuban tobacco known simply as Criollo (one of the English translations of which is 'native'). By the late 1930s it was widely planted in Cuba's prime plantations.

Corojo, a legendary strain of tobacco, was developed from careful cross-pollination of Criollo with Sumatra seed (the latter gave the hybrid an elasticity perfectly suited for

L
E
X
I
C
O
N

SEED

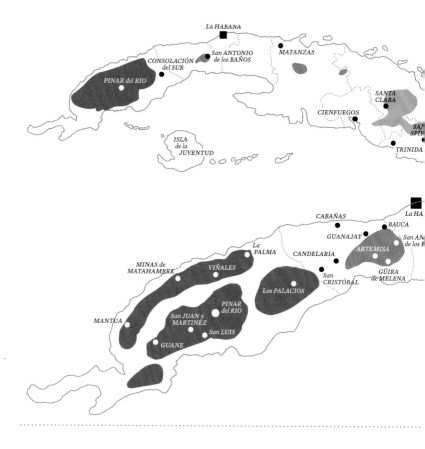

growth under shade cloth). [13] According to *Cigar Aficionado* magazine, Corojo is 'considered by many connoisseurs to be the finest tobacco ever grown in Cuba', [14] and respected cigar and wine writer James Suckling described it as 'the greatest wrapper tobacco in the world'. [15] It was developed in the 1940s by Diego Rodriguez, the owner of the Santa Ines del Corojo plantation in San Luis. Rodriguez had rented the plantation from the Allones family in 1920, and then added to

[13] Gordon Mott, 'A Passion for Seeds', *Cigar Aficionado*, July/August 2015

[14] http://www.cigaraficionado.com/webfeatures/show/id/3487, accessed 3 July 2016

[15] James Suckling, 'Cuba's Best Wrapper', *Cigar Aficionado*, Summer 1995

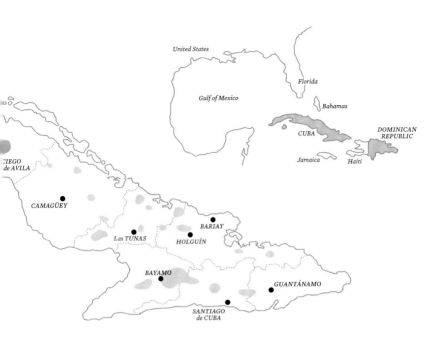

TOBACCO GROWING REGIONS OF CUBA

VUELTA ABAJO   REMEDIOS

PARTIDO   VUELTA ARRIBA

it with purchases of neighbouring properties that shared the same soil characteristics and microclimate until it covered 400 acres. It remains about the same size today.

Corojo subsequently became a cult among cigar lovers, and is an example of a tobacco seed that has established an identity among cigar smokers, just as grape varieties such as Cabernet Sauvignon and Pinot Noir have with oenophiles (many non-Cuban brands promote the variety as a brand in itself; Camacho and La Aurora both sell popular lines called Corojo). The Rodriguez family were among the many growers and cigar makers who left the island in 1960, but the plantation continues to enjoy a mythical status.

The original Corojo seed has been succeeded by varieties less susceptible to disease, such as Corojo 99 and Habano 2000. The latter, bred to supply wrapper leaf, was somewhat controversial, and, according to the revered Alejandro Robaina, a celebrated tobacco farmer [see page 192], flawed. 'I was the first to plant Habano 2000 here in Cuba and the results were very good,' he said in an interview in October 2006, 'but nowadays Habano 2000 has lost quality to the point that I am not planting it any more. It's prone to blue mold and black shank. Plus, there are now other seeds that have much better quality.'[16]

The retirement of Corojo in the mid-1990s coincided with a change in the character of Havana cigars, although whether this was in response to changing tastes or as a result of new seed strains is far from certain. At the time of the changeover, James Suckling commented: 'Pre-hybrid smokes could one day be likened to the pre-phylloxera wines of Europe that have a legendary reputation among great wine collectors. These are wines that were made primarily before 1880 from old, gnarly vines whose roots were anchored deep in the soil to extract an amazing amount of nutrients. They produced concentrated wine grapes with character. Unfortunately, they had not been grafted or spliced to American rootstock to protect them from the ravenous root louse that destroyed most of Europe's vineyards during the latter part of the nineteenth century.'[17]

[16] James Suckling, 'Cigar Diary: Cuba's Cigar Legend',
Cigar Aficionado website, posted 1 October 2006

[17] James Suckling, 'The Death of El Corojo', *Cigar Aficionado*,
July/August 2000: http://www.cigaraficionado.com/webfeatures/
show?id=7051, accessed 28 April 2016

By the second decade of the current century, Cuba had developed a range of seed varieties to combat specific climatic problems and diseases. Resistance to specific threats varies among seeds, and therefore they need to be selected very carefully in relation to the microclimate and historic susceptibility to disease of the growing area.

Other variables include the potential yield and leaf size. Thus there is no substitute for intimate knowledge of the land and the soil, as even different areas of the same plantation will demonstrate different characteristics, which may account for Robaina's insistence that small private farmers achieve better results than large state-owned farms, local knowledge and motivation being higher among private farmers, who in many cases grew up on the land they farm.

MAIN VARIETIES of CUBAN SEED [18]

Habano 2000

Originally developed as a replacement for original Corojo wrappers (although Robaina believed otherwise), Habano 2000 was designed to be resistant to black shank (*Phytophthora nicotianae Breda de Haan*), which rots roots and stems; brown spot (*Alternaria*), a fungal disease that covers leaves with brown spots; *Fusarium oxysporum*, a fungus that impedes water conduction to the leaves, leading to wilting and death; environmental necrosis; and blue mould, caused by the fungus *Peronospora tabacina*. However, it is susceptible to tobacco mosaic virus, which causes mottling and discoloration and stunts leaf growth; *Orobanche ramose*, a parasitic weed that 'steals' nutrients from tobacco plants; and tobacco budworm (*Heliothis virescens F.*), the larvae of which tunnel into blossoms and buds. Habano 2000 is used for shade-grown wrapper with much success outside Cuba.

[18] The section on Cuban seed draws upon various sources including the 2012 Tabacuba, Minsistry of Agriculture, Tobacco Research Institute paper 'Instructivo Tecnico para el Cultivo del Tabaco en Cuba,' Artemias 2012; and the Clemson University Extension Serivce, report *Tobacco Diseases: An Aid to Identification and Control*, 1997

Habano 92

Resistant to blue mould, black shank, environmental necrosis, fusarium and orobanche, this highly tolerant variety was developed as a hardy successor to the original Criollo and is characterised by leaves of an intense bright green. It is particularly resistant to drought: it can survive for long periods without water, and within 10 days can achieve the level of development of seed that has not been deprived of water. It is suitable for both sun and shade growing.

Criollo 98

Lower in height than other black tobacco plants while yielding the same number of leaves (16 per plant), Criollo 98 is resistant to blue mould and fusarium; moderately resistant to black shank and environmental necrosis; and susceptible to budworm. American cigar brand Alec Bradley launched a line of Criollo 98 cigars in 2001, followed by CAO's Criollo in 2002 also using this hybrid.

Corojo 99

Closely related to Criollo 98 but distinguished by larger, rounder leaves, Corojo 99 is a supremely versatile tobacco that flourishes both in and outside Cuba and can be sun- or shade-grown with equal success. It is resistant to blue mould, fusarium and tobacco mosaic and moderately resistant to black shank and environmental necrosis. However, it is susceptible to budworm and orobanche.

Sancti Spiritus 96

This rapidly growing high-yielding plant produces smooth leaves of a grey-green colour that grow at an acute angle from the stem. It is primarily grown in the central provinces of Cuba. It is resistant to blue mould and tobacco mosaic; moderately resistant to black shank and environmental necrosis; susceptible to budworm, orobanche and fusarium.

Corojo 2006

Resistant to blue mould, black shank, fusarium, tobacco mosaic and environmental necrosis, but susceptible to orobanche, with a potential yield of 2–6 tonnes per hectare, this variety is favoured in Cuba's eastern provinces, where sun-grown plants of up to 24 leaves are used for domestic production and cigarette manufacture. However, better quality is achieved with plants of around 18 leaves.

Criollo 2010

An androsterile hybrid variety that is resistant to blue mould, black shank, environmental necrosis, fusarium and tobacco mosaic, but susceptible to budworm and orobanche, Criollo 2010 is often used for wrapper, thanks to the large size of its leaves, the minimal veining when dry and the desirable colour range, but also makes filler and binder. An 18-leaf plant will yield around 2·2 tonnes per hectare, and is considered superior to Habano 2000 on account of its enhanced blue mould resistance and its capacity to flourish in a wide range of soil types.

Sancti Spíritus 2006

Resistant to black shank, blue mould, tobacco mosaic and fusarium, suiting it to planting in central areas where there is no shortage of water, this sun-grown tobacco is however susceptible to budworm and orobanche.

Habana Burley 13

Resistant to black shank and tobacco mosaic, moderately resistant to blue mould and fusarium, susceptible to orobanche, Habana Burley has a yield potential of 2·3 tonnes per hectare. There are 20 to 22 usable leaves per plant, with the largest having an average width of 30–34 cm and a length of 60–64 cm.

Burley Pinar 2004

Only slightly resistant to black shank etc., this variety was developed to be planted in areas prone to potato virus Y and tobacco etch virus, which engraves leaves with lines and causes mottling.

Burley Pinar 2010

More compact than the Habana Burley 13, and flowering about 10 days later, this variety is resistant to black shank, blue mould and fusarium, moderately resistant to environmental necrosis, and susceptible to budworm and orobanche. Its leaves can be characterised by a marked hyponasty, and there is good yield potential (2·25 tonnes /ha).

San Luis 21

Resistant to black shank, blue mould, environmental necrosis and fusarium, but susceptible to tobacco mosaic, budworm and orobanche, this variety has a high number of usable leaves (up to 24 per plant), but commercially best results are obtained when pruned to 18 or 20 leaves per plant.

San Luis 22

Resistant to black shank and fusarium; moderately resistant to blue mould; and susceptible to environmental necrosis, tobacco mosaic, budworm and orobanche, it has fewer usable leaves than San Luis 21, but they are much larger. Because of its comparatively low resistance to blue mould, cultivation is recommended early in the growing season to minimise exposure to the cool damp conditions that favour the disease.

Harvesting leaves in one of Davidoff's Dominican Republic plantations

Cuban seed has proliferated throughout the region since the revolution dispersed many cigar makers, farmers and leaf experts to other Caribbean and Central American countries. According to Davidoff's Henke Kelner, 10,000 seeds weigh one gramme, making them readily transportable. Knowing this, Davidoff breeds its seeds to be sterile so they cannot be pirated, and Henke, who runs arguably the best-resourced operation in the Dominican Republic, emphasises the importance of matching the right seed to the right soil. 'The most important thing is the combination of the seed with the soil. One seed and one soil yields one style of tobacco; but if you're growing that seed in another soil, the tobacco can be totally different. It depends on the condition and the composition of the soil.'[19]

Until the 1950s, the most common Dominican varieties were Quin Diaz, which has since fallen from use; and Olor, which often accounts for the characteristic salty or dry effect of Dominican cigars. Olor is blended with varieties that arrived in 1962, after the Cuban revolution: the Piloto Cubano, and a Piloto hybrid called San Vicente that was developed at the eponymous farm in the Vuelta Abajo. These are the three seeds that form the traditional foundations of Dominican cigar making. However, since the turn of the century, Davidoff has created numerous varieties, often with specific locations and soil compositions in mind, which are stored in a restricted area of the Jicomé facility in large, locked industrial fridges.

....

[19] Henke Kelner, interview with author, June 2016

Elsewhere in the region, Habano 2000 flourishes under the near-perpetual cloud cover of Ecuador, producing wrappers that are used all over the region; as does Connecticut seed. Criollo 98, Habano 2000, Habano 92, Corojo and Connecticut are planted in Nicaragua and Honduras, while on the other side of the Andes, protected by mountains from the pests that rendered it useless in its homeland, Pelo de Oro is grown in Peru.

SHADE-GROWN

[*See: TAPADO*, page 146]

SHAPES & SIZES

[*See also: VITOLA*, page 152, *RING GAUGE*, page 117,
ROBUSTO, page 118 and *TORPEDO*, page 147]

Sizing of cigars is a nightmare. Just as you think you have mastered the hundreds of different sizes that make up the production of Cuba alone, some cigars will be discontinued, new ones added, and a new crop of *LIMITED EDITIONS* [*q.v.,* page 94] will mean that this mentally held information needs to be updated. There is no easy way round it.

Some of the classic sizes, by their popular rather than factory names, are listed below, with the approximate time it takes to enjoy one, but even this incredibly simplistic overview presents difficulties: for example, a Canonazo will take about as long to work through as a Lancero, and yet two more different cigars it would be hard to imagine, the first a thick, chunky tube comprising up to four different filler leaves, rich in flavour, with which it saturates the palate; the second an elegant wand of tobacco to be smoked with grace and finesse. But then I suppose that this variety of experience is what accounts for the endless fascination of cigars.

Panetela
26 × 4½ in/115 mm · 10–15 minutes
Cohiba Panetela · Montecristo Joyita
Romeo y Julieta Petit Julieta

Perla
40 × 4 in/102 mm · 15–20 minutes
Montecristo No.5 · Cohiba Siglo I

Petit Robusto
50 × 4 in/102 mm · 20–25 minutes
Hoyo de Monterrey Petit Robusto
Romeo y Julieta Petit Churchill

Robusto
50 × 4⅞ in/124 mm · 40 minutes
Cohiba Robusto · Partágas Serie D No.4
Bolívar Royal Corona
Hoyo de Monterrey Epicure No.2
Montecristo Open Master
Ramón Allones Specially Selected
Davidoff Special R · Fuente Opus X Robusto
Alec Bradley Prensado
Camacho Connecticut Robusto

Petit Corona
42 × 5⅛ in/129 mm · 20–25 minutes
H. Upmann Petit Corona · Romeo y Julieta Cedros No.3
Montecristo No.4 · Cohiba Siglo II

Corona
42 × 5⅝ in/142 mm · 30 minutes
Montecristo No.3 · Romeo y Julieta Corona

Canonazo
52 × 5⅞ in/150 mm · 1 hour
Cohiba Siglo VI

Toro
a non-Cuban size that varies between
brands but is typically 52/54 × 6 in/152 mm · 1 hour
Davidoff Winston Churchill Commander · Padrón No.45

Torpedo
52 × 6⅛ in/156 mm · 1 hour
H. Upmann No.2 · Montecristo No.2
Davidoff Yamasa Pirámides

Lancero
38 × 7½ in/190 mm · 1 hour
Cohiba Lanceros · Montecristo Especial

Churchill
47 × 7 in/178 mm · 1 hour 10 minutes
Cohiba Esplendido · Romeo y Julieta Churchill
Davidoff Winston Churchill Aristocrat
H. Upmann Sir Winston

Double Corona
49 × 7⅝ in/194 mm · 1 hour 20 minutes
Partagás Lusitania
Hoyo de Monterrey Double Corona

A
47 × 9¼ in/240 mm · 2 hours
Sancho Panza Sancho · Montecristo A

SICK PERIOD

[*See*: *MATURATION*, page 96]

SLB

Slide lid box. Reminiscent of the pencil cases of my youth, the 'cabinet selection' is my personal favourite packing method. Bundles of 25 cigars are bound with ribbon and packed in the box. Occasionally the cigars that have been on the outer layer of the bundle will bear a slight declivity left by the ribbon.

HABANOS MARKINGS & LABELS

English Market Selection (EMS) stamp

Habanos S.A. chevron

Cuban Government warranty seal

UK health warning

'Hecho en Cuba' translates as 'Made in Cuba'

'Totalmente a Mano' translates as 'Totally by hand'

The two ink stamps on the bottom of the box indicate the factory where the cigars were made (in encrypted code) and the month and year when the cigars were boxed

SOIL

The rich soil of the Caribbean and Central America is ideally suited to the cultivation of cigar tobacco, but there are significant differences, which result in different behaviours of cigars: for instance, an ash of snowy whiteness is evidence of high levels of magnesium in the soil, often seen in Dominican cigars, whereas the lightest a Cuban ash will achieve is a silvery hue or remain on the cigar demonstrating a striated grey.

STAMPS, SEALS & STICKERS

As well as the inevitable and increasingly obvious health warnings, a Cuban cigar box is plastered with all sorts of other colourful labels until it resembles a piece of vintage luggage covered with hotel, airline and cruise ship labels. The most famous of these is the green and white warranty label bearing the words 'Republica de Cuba', which appears to be doing its best to mimic a banknote in appearance.

The warranty seal pre-dates the existence of the republic and was first introduced in 1889 by royal decree of the King of Spain. Given that Alfonso XIII was just three years old at the time, His Majesty was clearly precocious in his taste for the better things life had to offer.

The current design, featuring palm trees and the arms of the Republic of Cuba, dates from 1912. It was first modified in 1931, and again in 1999, with the addition of a red serial number and a marking visible only under ultraviolet light. Ten years after that, in 2009, it was changed again to incorporate further technology: bar code and hologram. The Cuban industry is particularly proud of its new seal; in its description of its powers, it makes it sound like it was developed by Q in a James Bond film, featuring among other things both self-destructive and, for good measure, auto-destructive capability.

> *This Seal has been developed through a base of synthetic paper with special characteristics such as an auto-destructive feature before any attempts at removal and with several maximum security techniques added:*
> - *NON-TRANSFERABLE LABEL*
>   *Any attempt to remove it will cause invalidation of the seal by self destruction.*
> - *HIGH ADHERENCE OF THE PAPER (PLASTIC)*
>   *Auto-destructive, Self-destructive.*
> - *SCAN- AND PHOTOCOPY-PROTECTED SYSTEM*
>   *The holographic band will show a bicolor text in 2nd and 3rd dimension.*
> - *ELEMENTS WITH OPTICAL VARIATIONS ATTACHED*
>   *Also it will enclose a micro dot only visible through laser scanner.'*[20]

However, if you have left your laser scanner at home and don't want to tamper with the self-destruct feature, then the position of the label on the box offers hints as to its authenticity: it is usually on the lower left-hand side, between 3 and 6 mm from the edge, and the Cuban Coat of Arms is usually placed over the opening of the box.

Since 1994, each box has also had to carry a rather

---

[20] http://www.habanos.com/en/verificacion-de-autenticidad/, accessed February 2016

gaudy black, white, yellow, red and gold Denominación de Origen Protegida sticker across the top right corner, emblazoned with the word 'Habanos'. This is the equivalent of the *appellation contrôlée* on a bottle of wine and no box is shipped from Cuba without it. Next to the DOP sticker there may also appear a further sticker if the box is a limited edition.

As well as information about the date and place of manufacture, the bottom of the box is hot-stamped with the Habanos SA logo (boxes made between 1985 and 1994 are stamped with its predecessor, Cubatabaco). 'HECHO EN CUBA' (made in Cuba) appears in a lozenge beneath which are the words 'Totalmente a Mano' (completely handmade); if these words are not there, the cigars inside will be machine-made.

STORAGE

The usual advice given on storing cigars is that the temperature should be between 16 and 18 degrees Celsius – any warmer and the risk of weevils [*q.v.*, page 153] increases – with

65–70 per cent relative humidity [*q.v.,* page 112] to stop the cigars drying out. Some noted connoisseurs prefer on occasion to smoke drier cigars stored at a lower relative humidity; however, I prefer to keep cigars at the 'correct' humidity, as I believe this maintains the aroma, assists with gentle ageing and maintains the natural oils that give the cigars their glossy sheen – dry a cigar too long or too much and the appearance, bouquet, flavour and aroma suffer.

There is no shortage of humidors on the market; even Dior, the couture, fashion and fragrance house, stocks some beautiful examples in its gifts and homeware department. When it comes to luxury humidors, Elie Bleu is the best-known maker, with a variety of exotic woods and decorative finishes. In 2016, the French marque reached a new summit of sophistication with the commemorative cabinet humidor created to house the 60 ring gauge Cohiba 50 Anniversario, crafted from a variety of exotic woods including macassar ebony, sycamore and scented guarea. The aesthetic highlight was the decoration of the doors with a marquetry technique 'in which carefully selected authentic ligero Vuelta Abajo leaves were coated with 24-carat gold leaf'.[21]

It was a far from straightforward job.

The work to create this marquetry was meticulous and highly complex: each leaf was carefully selected, not permitting any tears or other imperfections, as if it were being selected for the finest Habano in the world. After this, the best part of each leaf was chosen, which was then stuck to a wooden base to let it air dry for ten days, before cutting

[21] Cohiba 50 Aniversario, Habanos SA, 2016

into small squares. The requirements were so demanding that only one square per leaf was usually obtained.

Binding the gold leaf to the tobacco required unprecedented innovative solutions. The application, with silk brushes, demanded patience and meticulous care, with no margin for error. An insulation had to be applied over a period of three days in order to encapsulate and protect the golden leaves for the following phase of varnishing. Up to ten coats were applied to the doors and accessories before the final phase of polishing. [22]

As well as coming with a travel humidor, leather cigar case and matching ashtray, the humidor was equipped with some decidedly twenty-first-century gadgetry. 'This cabinet features a device that allows its owner to follow the temperature and humidity conditions in the humidor directly on their smartphone or tablet, thanks to an app that will be remotely connected to a sensor inside the humidor. The app will also be an exclusive communication channel for the brand's updates marking its 50th anniversary and will allow the owner to have a digital version of their certificate of ownership and authenticity.' [23]

I have yet to test this high-tech solution and I hope that it is an improvement on the majority of in-humidor hygrometers, which in my experience are erratic in their performance. In fact, for trouble-free storage of cigars I have found that I can rely on the minimally equipped clear plastic humidors made by Davidoff.

....

[22] Ibid.

[23] Ibid.

If you want to store cigars at home, there are special units that resemble wine fridges, and, like bottles of wine, you can also leave your cigars in the cellar too. However, for storing large numbers of boxes for extended periods, there is no substitute for long-term lodging with a respected and trusted cigar merchant.

At this point I must make mention of the highly sophisticated system that has been devised by the Birley Cigar Shop, attached to the fashionable London members' club 5 Hertford Street.

Although a relative newcomer to the London cigar scene, Birley have taken a highly scientific approach to long-term storage of cigars, developing what they call the Birley Technology for use in a secure vault located close to the Mayfair club. Traditionally cigars are aged at a lower temperature than the standard 16–18 degrees, but 5 Hertford Street believes that while this is successful at controlling weevil infestation, it places unnatural limits on the ageing process. As the system is new and includes machinery built especially for the ageing of cigars, these hypotheses will only be validated or otherwise over time. Nevertheless, the lengths to which Birley have gone to achieve what they regard as optimum conditions are highly impressive.

As relative humidity changes with air temperature, one of the system's most important features is:

an intelligent microprocessor that looks at both the Humidity and the Temperature simultaneously, constantly monitoring both functions. If the temperature starts to rise the unit will introduce cooling but only marginally by way of an inverter driven compressor, so rather than the compressor running at full speed it will run at a calculated percentage depending on the amount of required cooling. Before the space reaches the required set point the cooling will reduce and the unit will wait and assess the space conditions through 18 sensors positioned throughout the room.

This process stops the cooling function from 'overshooting' the desired amount which would then reduce the Relative Humidity percentage too far and cause the Humidifier to produce more humid air than it really needs to as would happen in the example of the traditional system. The Humidity function operates in the

Cigars ageing in the optimum conditions of the vault at Five Hertford Street

STORAGE

same way as the cooling function with the result being a
'precise' temperature and Relative Humidity condition.

The system's claimed control of relative humidity is to plus or minus 1 per cent and temperature to plus or minus 0·3°C. Such stability of temperature is remarkable and of course in turn makes the achievement of the correct relative humidity much easier. However, this was not sufficient for the company's maniacal attention to detail. Not unlike the tuck room I remember from my junior house at boarding school, the vault contains multiple lockers, or 'keeps', against the walls at different heights. However, unlike my school tuck room, they are beautifully finished by a skilled cabinetmaker and contain cigars rather than stale cake and chocolate. Within these lockers, collectors' boxes are stored; all at different levels and distances from the air supply. So 5 Hertford Street did what anyone would do in such a situation and constructed:

a 3D Airflow model to understand the journey of the
air particles, which led us to build rotary air supply
vents in the ceiling, allowing the air to be expelled in
a vortex into the room. Now the challenge was getting
this air into each locker at the required RH [relative
humidity] *level.*

This was finally achieved by creating a microclimate
within each locker at every level. So at the back of each
locker are a slide vent, an electronic hygrometer, and
motor fan. The electronic hygrometer measures the RH
required for each specific locker and the motor draws in
the RH to keep the lockers at the perfect RH and speed.
The speed of the air following inside a locker is vital and
must also be calculated, monitored and controlled, as

cigars do not like fast air flow, which can cause many issues to a cigar.

One last problem we had to tackle was the fresh air supply, which is a component of RH. We did not want a musty smell in our keeps room for those storing with us cigars of great value for many years, hence the introduction of various layers of filtered air to the unit was compulsory [apparently this required five different filters]. *This meant calculating the amount of air we needed to circulate in the room per hour as a component of density and volume, as well as purifying the air before it entered the machine to be cooled and humidified. The end result meant we achieved 98.8% clean surgical air.* [24]

According to 5 Hertford Street, this means that if the NHS ever wants to perform an operation in a centrally located secure cigar storage facility, then their air is of the required quality.

Those with cigars in storage can use a password to access the climatic readings of their locker and monitor both contents and microclimate. This data can be printed to provide provenance should the locker holder decide to sell the cigars – increasingly likely as cigar prices for certain rarities continue to rise.

Forget my cigars: from the sound of it I would benefit from long-term ageing in such perfectly controlled conditions; but alas, I cannot afford to provide this sort of wonderful environment for my cigars, let alone my family.

....

[24] Nadim Marrow, interview with the author, June 2016

STRING

In Cuba's so-called 'Special Period' after the collapse of the Soviet Union, shortages of basic commodities made life difficult, and during the early 1990s, harvests were adversely affected by a shortage of string. String is used to tie the tops of shade-grown tobacco plants to the cheesecloth canopy.

TAPADO

The Spanish term for 'shade-grown tobacco', cultivated under canopies of cheesecloth.

TORCEDOR

The Spanish word for 'cigar roller'. The chief difference between the Cuban and non-Cuban methods of rolling is that outside Cuba rollers tend to work in pairs, one using a bunching machine, a hand-operated device that prepares the filler, the other applying the wrapper leaf.

TORO

A term used to describe a longer Robusto [*q.v.*, page 118], usually applied to non-Cuban cigars.

A colloquialism and a misnomer that refers to almost any Figurado (shaped cigar). The most common sorts of Torpedo are the Belicoso, which has a pointed head and slopes gradually towards the foot of the cigar, and the Pirámide, which is straighter for longer and narrows to its point much higher up. If there is such a thing as a cigar that looks like a torpedo, it is probably the double Figurado (pointed at both ends and bulging towards the foot), the only cigar type made by the Cuaba brand.

In its various sizes and guises the Figurado is also known as a Salomon, a Diadema, a Rodolfo, a Romeo, a Pirámide Extra, a Petit Pirámide, a Campana, a Taco, an Exquisito, a Petit Bouquet, a Generoso, a Favorito, a Forum, a President, a Chisel, a Petit Belicoso and a Petit No.2. The largest of these is the zeppelin-like giant Perfecto known as the Diadema [shown actual size *below*], a little under 9¼ in/235 mm in length with a ring gauge at its widest point of 55, but my favourite is the slightly girthier Salomon, which measures 7¼ in/184 mm with a 57 ring gauge.

I remember that when I got into cigars in the early 1990s, practically speaking there were just two Figurados that were widely available: the Montecristo No.2 and the H. Upmann No.2. Numerical nomenclature was not the only thing that linked them; they were identically dimensioned (52 × 6⅛ in/155 mm). Moreover, in those days the dusty

brown bands were almost identical too, and depending on when they were made (the blend does change slightly from year to year), it was sometimes difficult to tell the difference between the slightly fuller-flavoured Monte and the allegedly more delicate Upmann. As I remember, they were primarily smoked by the likes of Lew Grade and by those of who wanted to have the experience of a slightly fatter cigar. In those days the 50 ring gauge Robusto was at the limit of girth in a straight-sided cigar and there were relatively few marques that offered it.

But to see it as just another fat cigar is to miss the point. In fact the point of a Pirámide or Perfecto is not the girth; the point is ... well ... the point. The flavour delivery of the Pirámide is unique in that it offers the complexity and nuanced blending that is afforded by having more tobacco in a wider ring gauge, in particular the inclusion of the slower-burning, more powerful *ligero*; but if cut correctly (a straight cut between 3½ and 4 mm from the top), it delivers its flavour with the intensity of a slimmer cigar, concentrating the initial taste to a smaller area of the palate. This configuration completely alters the character of the cigar, even within the same brand.

It is often observed that the shape of the Pirámide allows for better combustibility; however, this may not be solely to do with the geometry of the shape. Figurados are much more difficult to make than Parejos, as Lázaro Collazo,

Romeo y Julieta Pirámide Añejado

head of quality control at the Habanero factory in Havana province explained to me. 'The main challenge is in the "head" or *cabeza* of the cigar. In a Parejo cigar you cut the binder/filler after you have rolled a cylinder of tobacco. This creates the flat end onto which the cap is placed. With a Pirámides you have to continue rolling the binder and filler tobacco into a Pirámide shape and then also add the cap at the end. This is a more complicated and difficult process.'

Looking at the needle-sharp point of a good Pirámide, it is hard not to marvel at the manual dexterity that enables a top roller to repeat this precise feature time after time, using only hand, eye and experience. Grade 9 is the highest level of skill to which a *torcedor* can aspire, and only Grade 9 rollers are permitted to make the larger Figurados, (including Rodolfos, Pirámides and Pirámides Extra). Even the smaller Figurados, those between 4³⁄4 and 5¹⁄2 inches (120 and 140 mm) in length (Campana, Forum, Petit Pirámide, Petit Belicoso and Petit No.2) can only be tackled by a Grade 8 or 9. And while Grade 9 is the highest official grade, I recall that in one factory I visited a couple of years ago, the rollers selected to work on special projects were designated as the Brigade Pirámide; demonstrating the high regard in which the Figurado is held by the industry.

The Pirámide reached its apotheosis when the Montecristo No.2 was made into a Gran Reserva, using tobacco from the 2005 harvest. The Montecristo Gran Reserva was a richly satisfying, almost majestic cigar; the aged tobaccos smoothing away the liveliness of youth with a carpet of harmonious flavours. The other classic Pirámide, the H. Upmann No.2, became a Reserva in 2013 using tobacco from 2010.

In 2012, the Cohiba Pirámides Extra (54 × 6¹⁄4 in/ 160 mm) was launched, the first addition to the fuller-flavoured Linea Classica of the super-premium cigar brand since 1989. Again this was a highly significant launch. The Linea Classica is the foundation of the Cohiba brand, and the introduction of a new format into such a hallowed and classic range is not a decision lightly taken. I tasted the Pirámides Extra shortly after it was launched and found it docile, smooth and subtle. Subsequently, however, I have found it getting a little stronger and developing into something not to be trifled with.

At Montecristo, the No.2 has been joined by a smaller sibling, the Montecristo Petit No.2, a cigar tailored to the requirement for short yet substantial cigars. It keeps the

Analysis of some Havana Torpedo (Figurado) Shapes

SIZE	ROLLER GRADE	VITOLAS DE SALIDA
54 × 7¹⁄8 in/180 mm	9	San Cristóbal Muralla ('06–'11)
54 × 6¹⁄4 in/160 mm	9	Cohíba Pirámides Extra ('12)
52 × 6¹⁄8 in/156 mm	9	Montecristo No.2 ('35)
		H. Upmann No.2 ('50s)
		Partágas P 2 ('05 & LE '00)
		Vegas Robaina Unicos ('97)
		Diplomáticos No.2 ('60s)
		Cohíba Pirámides LE ('01 & '06)
		Hoyo Pirámides (LE '03)
		Cuaba Pirámides (LE '08)
52 × 5¹⁄2 in/140 mm	8	Romeo y Julieta Belicosos ('50s)
		San Cristóbal La Punta ('99)
		Bolívar Belicosos Finos ('50s)
		Sancho Panza Belicosos ('50s)
		Punch Serie d'Oro No.2 (LE '13)
46 × 5³⁄8 in/135 mm	8	Montecristo Open Regata ('09)
		Hoyo Short Hoyo Pirámides (LE '11)
50 × 5 in/127 mm	8	Romeo y Julieta Petit Pirámides (LE '05)
52 × 5 in/125 mm	8	Bolívar Petit Belicoso (LE '09)
52 × 4³⁄4 in/120 mm	8	Montecristo Petit No.2 ('13)
46 × 4 in/100 mm	7	Vegueros Mañanitas ('13)

52 ring gauge of its big brother but is almost an inch and a half shorter at 4³⁄₄ in/120 mm.

These high-profile launches have been accompanied by some interesting special-edition Figurados; among them the Perfecto Bolívar Britanica Extra, and the Ramón Allones Pctit Belicoso, both regional editions for the UK of 2011 and 2012 respectively. Other short-production-run Figurados include limited editions such as the Punch Serie d'Oro No.2 of 2013; and the Hoyo Short Pirámides of 2011.

TRIPA

Tripa Larga (long filler) cigars are made using whole leaves, arranged in the cigar as they are on the plant, with the tip of the leaf at one end and the stem at the end that is clipped.

Tripa Corta (short filler), made from chopped leaf and leftovers from Tripa Larga cigars, tend to be more rustic smokes, such as Vegueros and José L. Piedra. There has been a valiant attempt to compare them to hearty French country wines from obscure *appellations contrôlées* – which does not do French country wines any favours. Faced with a Tripa Corta or nothing, I would choose the latter. Unless you absolutely positively have to have a cigar and can find nothing else, I would avoid them, as they cannot be accused of acting as a showcase of Cuban excellence.

TUBES

In 1933, Waldo Braden invented the aluminium cigar tube (subsequently tubes were equipped with a screw top and now many adopt a sliding trombone-like system). In Braden's original design, a tab-style opening rendered the tube unfit for reuse; apparently he was paranoid that unscrupulous individuals might replace the Upmann inside with an inferior cigar.

But even if he had not come up with a near-perfect method of maintaining a cigar in optimum condition, Braden would have entered cigar lore anyway as the man who pulled a gun in the boardroom. It was 1935, and J. Frankau & Co. [*see HUNTERS & FRANKAU*, page 89] had been bought from Braden & Stark by D. G. Freeman. Waldo was so opposed to the sale that he tried every means to stop it, and even went as far as stealing and hiding the company seal. When Freeman discovered that Waldo had been adding a hidden margin to the cigar tube sales, he sacked him.

VEGAS de PRIMERA

Tobacco plantations, which are confirmed as best cigar tobacco growing regions by the Cuban tobacco Institute.

VISO

[*See*: *LEAF*, page 92]

VITOLA

Vitola is the size and shape of a cigar; in Cuba, the *vitola de galera* refers to the generic factory name for a given size. The *vitola de salida* is the name on the box.

There is also what I feel should be called a *vitola popular*, by which the cigar will often be widely known. For example, a Partagás Lusitania (*vitola de salida*), is a

Prominente *(vitola de galera)* but most people know it as a Double Corona (49 × 7⁵⁄8 in/194 mm).

VOLADO

[*See*: *LEAF*, page 92]

WEEVILS

Among the worst nightmares of the cigar lover is weevil infestation; these tiny little creatures hatch inside the cigar and burrow perfectly circular pin-like holes through the sides. Further evidence of their unwelcome presence comes if, on tapping the foot of the cigar, a fine dark powder falls out: weevil excrement ... eugh! However, beetles only hatch when temperature and relative humidity rise above 22°C and 72 per cent respectively.

I don't fancy smoking weevil dung, so if I find a pinhole in a cigar I discard it and examine those in the same box or humidor forensically. If they are free of holes, I place them in a bag in the freezer for three or four days and then move them into the fridge before returning them to room temperature. As a precaution, since 2005 all Havana cigars have been frozen before leaving the island.

BRANDS

⟨ *BOLÍVAR* ⟩

Simón Bolívar, the brand eponym, was a pretty vigorous chap, achieving mythical status as the man who threw off the yoke of imperial Spain. His record as a liberator is impressive: in 1821 he freed his native Venezuela; a year later he made it a hat-trick, liberating Colombia and Ecuador; he seems to have taken a year off in 1823, but 1824 saw him back on form bringing freedom to Peru, adding Upper Peru (today known as Bolivia – he had a country as a well as a cigar brand named in his honour) to his score-card a year later.

Thus he was an apposite choice of brand name for a cigar launched in 1902, after Cuba had kicked out the Spaniards, ending just over four centuries' rule of the island from Madrid; and doubtless the J. Rocha Company, which made such resolutely Hispanic brands as El Crepusculo, wanted to explore the possibilities of exporting cigars to markets other than Spain.

With its vast empire and its new, cigar-smoking king, Edward VII, England must have presented amazing opportunities to the astute cigar producer, but the right name had to be found. Happily, as well as being a liberator, Bolívar was something of an Anglophile: the inscription on his statue in Belgrave Square reads, 'I am convinced that England alone is capable of protecting the world's precious rights as she is great, glorious and wise.'

Like the man himself, the cigars have a powerful presence. I daresay this nineteenth-century Che Guevara was a macho character, and the cigars are similarly styled. Their flavour is robust and forceful. The names of the various sizes bristle with Latin machismo: Immensas, Belicosos Finos and the fabled Coronas Gigantes.

Bolívars tend to be rich, earthy and a bit too much of a test of one's masculinity for my liking; it is a cigar that needs to be wrestled into submission. If you have the cojones and the palate, try the Coronas Gigantes, the closest thing Cuba has produced to a weapon of mass destruction since the Missile Crisis of 1962. If you have ever seen one of those films about the Second World War in which, with a great clanking rumble, the wall of a house collapses like damp cardboard as a giant Tiger tank drives through the bricks and mortar without so much as a gear change, then you will have an idea how some of the strongest Bolívars can taste. This is a subjective view: but the least successful Bolívars allow strength to triumph at the expense of flavour, delivering a crushing steamroller of strength without nuance that subdues rather than seduces the palate.

They tend not to be cigars for the neophyte. Of all Cuban marques it is fair to say that Bolívar is the most powerful, and it is therefore hardly surprising that since the 1950s Bolívar cigars have been made alongside Partagás, another fuller-flavoured Havana. The rich, unique flavour is not derived from a higher-than-usual proportion of *ligero* leaf; rather, more *seco* than *volado* is used in the blend than in the Partagás.

But the Cuban cigar industry is nothing if not full of apparent contradictions, so I suppose I should not have been surprised to find that Bolívar once made the smallest Havana, the Delgado (under 2 inches in length and with a slender 20 ring gauge), and that the wide Churchill format Bolívar Belgravia that was released as a regional edition in the UK in 2015 was uncharacteristically approachable and almost smooth, like a strong Romeo y Julieta. But in most cases, handle with care.

STRENGTH: Strong to overpowering, favouring presence over character

FLAVOUR: Earthy

CHARACTER: Like a wrecking ball, or a brick through a plate-glass window – hard to ignore

BEST ENJOYED: After a heavy meal (preferably a spicy curry) and before a long lie down

Packing Cohiba Behikes at Cohiba fatory

Today the black, white and egg-yolk yellow of the Cohiba is an axiom of modern good living that has taken its place alongside the Calatrava cross of Patek Philippe and the distinctive shadowed and serifed red lettering of Chateau Pétrus. I still remember my excitement at coming across it for the first time at the beginning of the 1990s. I was of course familiar with Montecristo and Davidoff, but this was something different; for a start, the band was straight-edged rather than swelling to a lozenge in the middle, and instead of the paper-covered box with the elaborate nine-teenth-century-style illustrations of star-crossed lovers or South American liberators, this was a varnished box, either hinged or with a sliding lid, branded with distinctive block lettering and the Taino head.

The beginnings of the Cohiba story are wreathed in myth and cigar smoke. At one time the creation of this most celebrated Cuban marque was ascribed to Che Guevara himself. Today the cigar's exact origins have been traced back to 1963. The cloud of nuclear doom that had hovered over the Caribbean during the tense days of the Missile Crisis had cleared and the sunlit uplands of Cuban socialism beckoned. Once again a man could enjoy a cigar in peace without fear of being interrupted by nuclear Armageddon.

Thus Castro's driver and chief bodyguard, Bienvenido Pérez Salazar, or 'Chicho', was sitting in El Commandante's

B
R
A
N
D
S

Oldsmobile enjoying a cigar rolled for him by a friend. Long, thin, elegant and distinguished by a little twisted pigtail of tobacco leaf at the end, it tasted as good as it looked. Castro was so impressed by the lingering aroma that Chicho offered him one. El Commandante enjoyed it enough to have its roller, Eduardo Rivera, summoned from his *torcedor*'s bench and entrusted with the solemn responsibility of rolling the leader's cigars.

At the time, Rivera was working in the old La Corona factory. Had I known a little more about the history of the Cohiba when the old factory was still open, I might have been tempted to ask my *torcedor* friend Taboada if he had known Rivera, and if he had been at his bench that day when the announcement crackled over the loudspeaker instructing Rivera to make his way to the factory entrance, where a comrade in military fatigues was waiting to take him to a top-secret meeting.

At this meeting, Rivera's friend Chicho asked him to roll some more of the delicious cigars. At first he thought he was just making cigars for a friend, but soon these slender sticks of tobacco became an indispensable revolutionary accessory, as much of a part of the look as luxuriant facial hair, heavy boots and olive-green military fatigues.

Ernesto 'Che' Guevara, the poster boy of radical chic, the man who adorned thousands of student bedsits in the 1960s and 1970s, claimed never to have smoked a better cigar, and it is said that even after he left the island to export the revolution to Bolivia, he was sent supplies of his favourite Cohibas.

For security reasons Rivera was moved between factories and sometimes rolled cigars at home. When a factory was established to make El Commandante's cigars, it was a high-security site. To this day an aura of secrecy still surrounds the brand: its home factory remains by far the most difficult cigar factory to visit.

The Cohiba was a genuine tool of the revolution. The cigar that we know today as the Lancero, a long Panetela of just over 7½ in/190 mm with a ring gauge of 38, became something of an ambassador for the country. An example of soft power, it was used as a diplomatic gift, presented with a personal band, with the likes of Marshal Tito of Yugoslavia and Colonel Nasser of Egypt among the lucky recipients.

In order to demonstrate the equality of the revolution, it was decreed that women would be trained as rollers to make these cigars. It was another woman, Celia Sánchez, the 'Flower of the Revolution', who took the Taino Indian word for the bunched leaves of tobacco that Columbus had seen being enjoyed by the island's inhabitants on his arrival and used it to name the new cigar Cohiba.

The cigar now had a name and a workforce, and in 1967 it moved into its current premises, in the former country club district of Havana: a sprawling mansion once belonging to a British treacle tycoon, a building that looks like it cannot quite make up its mind whether it wants to be Le Petit Trianon or just an oversized wedding cake. Called El Laguito, it has been immortalised in the name of the long, thin cigar that was the first Cohiba – Laguito No.1.

According to the official history, *We Shall Call them Cohiba* by Adargelio Garrido de la Grana, 'The first Cohiba brand design was used for a very short time.' Created in 1969, the design of the packaging, which used a stylised tobacco leaf motif repeated to create a semicircular fan that recalled the arches of colonial-era architecture, was judged politically incorrect. 'It was considered as portraying a concept far removed from that desired, due to the prominence of the colonial over the indigenous.'[11] The second design therefore stressed modernity and authenticity, with a graphic representation of a Taino head in profile against a tobacco leaf. It was not until the 1980s, however, that Cohiba was finally distributed outside Cuba, under a new livery and in just three sizes: Lanceros, Coronas Especiales and Panetelas.

During the eighties, cigar tastes tended to the long and slender, of which the Lancero was the epitome. The invention of the Cohiba Robusto [*above*] was a landmark in the history of the modern cigar. Today it is arguably the most famous cigar of what would become known as the Linea Classica of Cohiba, although its introduction to the market at the time was sotto voce. However, when it launched in 1989, just 25,000 were made for the whole world. With its 50 ring gauge, I remember it seeming an unconscionably indulgent cigar; in a ribbon-bound bundle of 25 cigars, their oily toffee-coloured wrappers almost glowing, it was incredibly seductive. Even so, it took me some time to work up the courage to tackle one. I feared the strength, but I need not have done so, as the power

[11]   Adargelio Garrido de la Grana, *We Shall Call them Cohiba* (Habanos SA, 1997), p.76

was like that delivered by the effortlessly turbocharged V8 of a Bentley: smooth and controlled thanks to the additional period of fermentation undergone by the *seco* and *ligero* leaves, lowering the nicotine and acidity. The quality and character of the Cohiba is further safeguarded by the fact that the tobacco used in the blend is harvested from what are considered the five best plantations in the Vuelta Abajo: La Perla and Santa Damiana in San Juan y Martinez; and Cuchillas de Barbacoa, La Fe and El Corojo in San Luis.

I was at the dinner at Claridge's in November 1993 where the Linea 1492 range of Cohibas was launched, the successor to the Cuban Davidoffs that had been made at El Laguito. The new range, Siglos I–V (one for each century since the arrival of Columbus in the New World), promised a slightly lighter style, and the Corona Gorda-sized Siglo IV (46 ring gauge × just over 5½ in/140 mm) became a rival to the Robusto in my affections.

Over time, the Cohiba has adapted to meet changing tastes. Today of course the taste is for ever girthier cigars, so a Siglo VI (52 ring gauge × just under 6 in/152 mm) was added to the Linea 1492. Reflecting the widespread acceptance of darker wrappers (viz. the popularity of the annual limited editions), 2007 saw the arrival of the Linea Maduro 5, the number referring to the five years' maturation of the dark, slightly sweet wrappers. In 2010 a new level of excellence was achieved with the arrival of the Linea Behike. It is the famous medio tiempo tobacco that gives the Behike range its unique potency.

But while these are rich and flavourful cigars, their large ring gauges, 52, 54 and the hard-to-manage 56, mean that the blenders have a bigger canvas on which to work and balance the flavours to provide an experience that at best is close to sublime. I say close, because of course the best cigar so far of this century is actually sublime: the Cohiba Sublime, a highly sought-after limited edition from 2004, although the Cohiba 1966 limited edition of 2011 comes a very close second.

Of course not every Cohiba has been brilliant, but given that when you include the limited runs and special editions there are around three dozen different varieties where there used only to be three, it is little short of miraculous (given the difficulties that the Cuban cigar industry has to face) that they are as consistently enjoyable as they are.

Cohiba Linea Classica

STRENGTH: The strong end of medium, with the narrow ring gauges packing surprising intensity

FLAVOUR: Spicy

CHARACTER: Elegant and assured

BEST ENJOYED: Relaxing in the back seat of a classic Oldsmobile after the Cuban Missile Crisis

Cohiba La Linea 1492

STRENGTH: Offically billed as medium, I would argue that the Siglo VI leans towards punchy

FLAVOUR: Dark chocolate with creamy overtones

CHARACTER: Elegant and refined

BEST ENJOYED: As a gateway to the Cohiba family

STRENGTH: Medium, but the dark wrapper makes it look stronger

FLAVOUR: Rich with a hint of eucalyptus

CHARACTER: Out of the strong comes forth sweetness

BEST ENJOYED: Instead of pudding

Cohiba Linea Behike

STRENGTH: If it were not so well balanced it would be a knockout

FLAVOUR: With these leaves and ring gauges it is like a kaleidoscope across the palate

CHARACTER: Hardly discreet but delicious

BEST ENJOYED: When you have plenty of time

❮ *CUABA* ❯

Back at the height of the first cigar boom in the nineteenth century, there was a craze for the Double Figurado – or what is colloquially known as a Double-Ended Torpedo. The end to be clipped widens gently into the main body of the cigar, which tapers to another pointed end that has a hole of a few millimetres diameter. Thanks to this construction, when the cigar is being lit, it produces a striking scimitar-shaped flame. A Double Figurado is one of the sternest tests of a roller's capability, and is therefore made by the most experienced hands, so chances are better than average that your Double Figurado will be neither under- nor overfilled; it will be free of blockages and will burn easily and evenly.

Introduced in 1996, the Cuaba range comprises only Double Figurados. At the time of their launch, one of the accessories available for customers to buy was a special tasselled velvet smoking cap of the type that Victorian patriarchs used to wear with smoking jackets to avoid their hair smelling too strongly of tobacco. If the nineteenth-century-inspired *vitolas* strike you as retro, then the name has roots even further in the past: *cuaba* was the Taino word for a readily combustible bush that they used to light their *tabacos*.

STRENGTH: Strong to overpowering, sometimes favouring presence over character

FLAVOUR: Rich roasted coffee beans

CHARACTER: Eccentric

BEST ENJOYED: In a velvet smoking hat, reading the latest work by the popular novelist Mr Charles Dickens

⟨ EL REY *del* MUNDO ⟩

Calling your brand King of the World is hardly self-effacing, but when Antonio Allones, launched (or according to some sources relaunched) the brand in 1882, his aim was to give the world a cigar whose excellence was reflected in its price, hence such similarly modest naming of the flagship cigar, Choix Supreme, a classic Hermoso No. 4 (or near Robusto). Allones was a towering figure in the nineteenth-century cigar trade, and even owned the fabled El Corojo plantation where the seed of the same name would be developed.

I have a real soft spot for El Rey del Mundo; it is arguably the perfect mild cigar, sophisticated, elegant and alas hard to find, as the range is much depleted from the days when it included the legendary Churchill-sized Taino.

STRENGTH: Mild

FLAVOUR: Delicate

CHARACTER: Distinguished

BEST ENJOYED: During the day (this is not a cigar that presents well after dinner)

⟨ H. UPMANN ⟩

Herman Upmann was a German banker who moved to Cuba in 1844 to found a bank and a cigar brand. The cigars proved more long-lived than the bank, which shut in the early 1920s.

In 1925, the brand and the factory passed into the hands of its UK distributor, J. Frankau & Co. Ltd. In 1935 it was bought by D. G. Freeman, great-grandfather of Jemma Freeman, owner of the UK Havana importers Hunters & Frankau [*see* page 89]. It remained in British ownership until 1937, when it was acquired for £100,000 by Menéndez, García y Cia, owners of the then recently launched Montecristo brand.

The circumstances of the sale were particularly colourful even by the standards of Havana in the thirties. An agreement was finally reached after 11 days of protracted, brandy-sodden negotiations, which commenced in a bar called the Reguladora opposite the H. Upmann factory, continued aboard an ocean liner that had been boarded inadvertently during the course of the deal-making, and concluded in New York.

H. Upmann is an ideal Havana brand for the neophyte cigar smoker, as it is widely regarded as one of the lightest; sometimes so light that for the more seasoned Havanaphile, smoking certain Upmanns seems merely like allowing warmed air to move across the palate. It was just such a cigar, the now discontinued Petit Upmann, that Kennedy famously asked his press secretary to buy in bulk before he signed the embargo on trade with Havana.

It is with the bigger cigars that the brand is best experienced, for instance the Churchill-sized Sir Winston. Recent years have seen some excellent arrivals: the Magnum 50, which was such a success as an Edición Limitada in 2005 that it was introduced to the main range in 2008; and the Connoisseur A, a longer (5½ in/140 mm), girthier (52 ring gauge) and more flavoursome counterpart to the 48 ring gauge 5 in/127 mm and reliably agreeable Connoisseur No.1.

STRENGTH: Mild

FLAVOUR: Generally smooth

CHARACTER: Sometimes delicate and docile; always accessible

BEST ENJOYED: After a light picnic lunch on a warm day

⟨ *HOYO de MONTERREY* ⟩

Its name is that of one of the great *vegas de primera* (first-class plantations) of the Vuelta Abajo, where there is a gateway inscribed with the words 'Hoyo de Monterrey José Gener 1860'.

Thirteen-year-old José Gener arrived from Spain in 1831 to work on an uncle's tobacco plantation. This was the beginning of what might be called the cigar rush, when great fortunes were to be made, and by the time he was in his thirties, Gener had his own factory and his own brand of cigars, La Escepción. By 1860 he had made enough money to consider acquiring his own plantation, and in buying what in Bordeaux would be one of the great classified growths, he entered the ranks of the major tobacco barons of the golden age of cigar making. Hoyo de Monterrey the brand first appeared in 1865, and by the turn of the century the Hoyo factory was the largest in Cuba, making a staggering 50 million cigars a year. In 1931, the brand passed into the hands of the owners of Punch [*q.v.*, page 179], and the two celebrated names have been stablemates ever since, complementing each other beautifully.

Hoyo used to be classed as a medium-strength cigar, but these days the tendency is to view it as light; indeed, a recent Petit Robusto [*overleaf*] came across as flirty with a hint of grassiness. Hoyo is most famous for its Double Coronas, one of the great cigars of all time: light, almost

B
R
A
N
D
S

sweet, certainly soft and yet complex and structured. It is one of the most approachable Cuban Double Coronas for the neophyte, and for the seasoned palate it is an excellent cigar with which to fill that gap between lunch and cocktails.

On the subject of seasoned palates, Hoyo de Monterrey has the honour of being the favoured marque of the second most famous British cigar smoker, Sir Terence Conran, who practically lives on a diet of black coffee and an endless supply of the Robusto-sized Hoyo de Monterrey Epicure No.2. Just as the Churchill has been shortened, widened and what-have-you at Romeo, so Hoyo has turned the Epicure name into a brand within a brand. Whereas once they used to appear unbanded in cabinets of 25, now Epicures Nos. 1 and 2 have two bands, one telling the world that the cigar is a Hoyo, and a second white band proclaiming its status as an Epicure. In 2008 they were joined by the Gordito-sized Epicure Especial (50 × 5½ in/140 mm).

Traditionally viewed as slightly stronger than the main range, the Le Hoyo series was created for a Swiss importer, A. Durr & Co. They are an interesting addition to the Hoyo range in that they are generally slender ring gauge cigars.

The slimmest, the Du Gourmet, is a superb example of what a long, slim (33 × 6¾ in/170 mm) cigar can be. It ages

Hoyo de Monterrey Petit Robusto

spectacularly, as I discovered when I ignited one from the late 1990s. It was a revelation. The time-smoothed flavours were apparent from the moment the flame licked the end of the cigar – instead of that initial burst of liveliness that may or may not settle down after a few puffs, I had this wonderful sense of toasted almonds, a warm, nutty character. It then developed a fullness that seemed almost out of place in such a slender cigar. A faint hint of cracked pepper crept across the palate, and there was body, structure and a characteristic that I can only describe imperfectly as the sort of biscuitiness that I used to experience with a good champagne. The last third developed a surprising richness, ending with a satisfying tang. It was not the strongest cigar I had ever smoked – think of a glass of *rosé* taken at lunch on the Côte d'Azur – but it was a complete cigar in that it developed, changed and revealed different facets of its character over the course of the half an hour I spent in its company.

The heaviest ring gauge in the Le Hoyo range was just 42 until 2014, when a Robusto Extra (54 × 5⁷⁄₈ in/150 mm) called Le Hoyo de San Juan was added. This is an interesting cigar in that it was to be made at a single factory rather than have its production spread across numerous locations, as well as because the *seco* and *ligero* in the blend come exclusively from the San Juan y Martínez DOP.

STRENGTH: Mild to medium

FLAVOUR: Smooth, nutty and grassy

CHARACTER: Sophisticated

BEST ENJOYED: In the company of Sir Terence Conran

⟨ *JOSÉ L. PIEDRA* ⟩

A brand of academic rather than epicurean interest – these rustic short filler cigars are made with tobacco grown exclusively in the Remedios region (once known as the Vuelta Arriba) – the perfunctory band and rustic nomenclature, i.e. Cazadores (hunter), suggest a bucolic nature that is duly delivered. It was once explained to me that this cigar was intended to be like a stout country wine; if so, it is one of those wines that taste good enough on holiday but do not travel well.

STRENGTH: Medium to full

FLAVOUR: Earthy and bitter

CHARACTER: Country yokel

BEST ENJOYED: By someone else

⟨ *La FLOR de CANO* ⟩

When I first became interested in cigars, the Flor de Cano Short Churchill was a cult. Robustos were rare, and this smooth and creamy cabinet selection cigar perfectly matched the tastes of the times, when cigars were not intended to deliver a blast of strength and youthful flavour and a 50 ring gauge was considered hefty. Of course, given the cigar's incredible popularity and its excellence, the Cubans did the obvious thing and discontinued it in the early 1990s.

Recent attempts to revive the lustre of the name with regional editions for Britain and Canada have not been triumphant – hardly helped by the fact that Romeo y Julieta has pinched the Short Churchill name for itself.

La Flor de Cano has a bit of an identity crisis, as it is known for producing a great many machine-made cigars up until 2002, when they were phased out in favour of short filler cigars, albeit hand-made.

STRENGTH: Adequate

FLAVOUR: Nondescript

CHARACTER: Inoffensive

BEST ENJOYED: In the late 1980s and early 1990s when the legendary Short Churchill was being made

⟨ MONTECRISTO ⟩

Although there are older Havana brands, there is none better known. The origin of the name is said to derive from the fact that Dumas' nineteenth-century blockbuster novel was a favourite of the *torcedores* in the Particulares factory where this brand was first made in the summer of 1935. It is not that literacy was so widespread in pre-revolutionary Havana, but rather that rollers were traditionally entertained as they worked by being read to by a lector.

The Particulares factory belonged to Alonso Menendez, scion of a family that emigrated from Spain to Cuba in 1890. A leaf tobacco specialist, he had found success as a maker with his brands Particulares and Byron, which were particularly popular in Britain, the largest market in the world for Havana cigars at that time.

With Montecristo, Menendez wanted to create a new brand of exceptional quality. He went into partnership with José Manuel 'Pepé' García, formerly a senior commercial manager at the Partagás factory, and in 1936 they founded the legendary Menendez y García company.

Working closely with the British cigar importers John Hunter, Morris & Elkan Ltd, whose managing director, Jack Benham, is said to have come up with the design of the Montecristo box, a relationship was formed with Alfred Dunhill Ltd, which sold the brand at its London and New York stores. The guiding principles for Montecristo were that production would be low, prices high and quality the finest. Distribution was selective, and whereas contemporary trade price lists show other brands listed and priced in full, Montecristo was strictly 'Price on Application'.

In 1937, Menendez, García y Cia bought the H. Upmann factory in Havana from its British owner, D. G. Freeman, and that year production of Montecristo was moved to H. Upmann, where it has remained ever since, although the location of the factory has changed more than once. The similarity between the brands even extended to the bands: from the 1960s until

Montecristo No.2 Pirámides

2006, the H. Upmann bands were the same umber colour and discreet size and shape as Montecristo's.

After the Cuban revolution in 1959, Alonso and Pepé set up a cigar business in the Canary Islands, and during the 1960s, factory floor manager José Manuel González, known as 'Masinguila', was credited with maintaining the continuity and consistency of the brand in Havana. In 1971, four new sizes were introduced: the 9¼ inch Montecristo A, the slender Especial and Especial No.2, and the Panetela-sized Joyita. During the 1970s in the UK, the Montecristo A, a telegraph pole of a cigar was considered the *ne plus ultra* of Havanas.

Since then, Montecristo has been overtaken in terms of prestige by other marques, but its reputation for consistency remains. Today almost a quarter of the Havana cigars sold in the UK are Montecristos of some sort or another; the country's favourite Havana is the Montecristo No. 4, which while not the most exciting cigar is usually dependable.

Indeed, for many years the brand, with its famous fleur-de-lis and épée motif was more reliable than rip-roaringly exciting; the medium-strength bittersweet tang seemed to deliver what many cigar lovers wanted from a smoke, and as nothing was broken, Habanos SA felt no need to fix anything until 2004, when, taking the name of Edmundo Dantès, hero of Dumas' novel, the Edmundo became the first size to be added to Montecristo's standard range since 1971. Measuring 52 × 5⅜ in/135 mm, the Edmundo was an entirely new *vitola de galera* (factory size) and only the second new 52 ring gauge Parejo (straight-sided) size to be introduced, less than a year after the Cohiba Siglo VI launched in June 2003. The Edmundo put Montecristo into the vanguard of the early twenty-first-century taste for ever-heavier ring gauges. It was soon joined by the stumpy Petit Edmundo, which packs a commendable amount of flavour into its 4³⁄₈ in/110 mm, and in 2013 by the Double Edmundo.

Montecristo Open, a sub-brand with a lighter flavour apparently aimed at younger smokers, was added in 2009. It must be doing the right thing as I, an older man, do not much care for it.

STRENGTH: Medium; on occasion full

FLAVOUR: Tangy and agreeably astringent

CHARACTER: Dependable

BEST ENJOYED: Any time, any place, anywhere
(local legislation permitting)

⊰ PARTAGÁS ⊱

Jaime Partagás was nothing if not precocious. The son of a Catalan tailor, he set sail for Cuba in the summer of 1831, aged just 14. He opened his eponymous factory in 1845.

Today the Partagás factory at 520 Industria (just behind the Cuban Capitol) is one of Havana's chief tourist attractions. Its lively cigar shop and smoking room, the latter equipped with the sort of large leather sofas that engulf the sitter, are meeting places for enthusiasts.

But just because this fine old building is on the tourist trail and you will have to fight your way through the heaving crowds in the shop to reach the almost-as-crowded smoking divan, it does not necessarily follow that Partagás cigars are just for tourists who wouldn't be able to tell a decent smoke from a poke in the eye with a sharp stick.

The brand tends towards strength and spiciness, and has the sort of structure that lends itself to ageing well. If it were a wine, it would have something of the 'farmyard' quality of a good Burgundy.

Notable cigars include the Serie D No. 4, probably the first Robusto. The Lusitania is a classic Double Corona, and although the *vitola* is less fashionable than it was in the late twentieth-century, this is a cigar that warrants inclusion in any humidor that likes to consider itself well stocked. The espresso-like Partagás Short was a favourite of the late taste maven and *arbiter elegantiarum* Mark Birley, and it if it was good enough for Mark then it is more than good enough for the rest of us. More recently the Partagás Maduro, a 2015 launch, has been well received: a Robusto-sized take on the dark-wrapper look that is absolutely delicious, with the traditional Partagás strength mediated by the sweetness imparted by the wrapper. The cigar comes with a bit too much bling in the form of an extra band and slightly fancier packaging, but don't let that put you off.

The most eccentric Partagás is the Culebras [*above*]. More a souvenir than a cigar, these three cigars plaited together and bound with string used to be machine-made but for the last 10 years or so have been hand-made using long filler. This unusual format references the daily ration of three cigars that was issued to cigar rollers and which they received in plaited bundles to distinguish them from the commercial production; thus a worker caught smoking a cigar that was not shaped like a corkscrew had probably 'liberated' it from the bench. The move to hand-made is an improvement; even so, they look more interesting than they taste.

STRENGTH: Verging on the fiery

FLAVOUR: Paprika, chilli and other spice

CHARACTER: Feisty

BEST ENJOYED: On a full stomach

POR LARRAÑAGA

The Petit Corona with the gold band, described as 'the standard bearer'[2] of the Por Larrañaga brand, does not cover itself in glory. A slightly harsh little stub of a thing, this

[2]   *UK Havana Cigar Portfolio*, second edn, p.66

178

is rather the little drummer boy attached to the regiment who does his best under the circumstances.

Far more interesting are the regional editions, among which the Por Larrañaga Magnifico (50 × 6³/₄ in/170 mm), released in 2007, is regarded as historically important. If there is a box to be ticked, the Magnifico ticks it, including a fancy old-style band. The cigar has aged very well and has a sweet flavour with a hint of liquorice, balanced, harmonious and satisfying. The Por Larrañaga Sobrasalientes of 2014 is almost as good and the brand has been chosen to make regional editions in many mainland European countries as well.

STRENGTH: Mild to medium

FLAVOUR: Smooth and creamy

CHARACTER: Harmonious

BEST ENJOYED: As a Regional Edition rather than the standard range

❮ PUNCH ❯

One of the great brands of Havana, founded in the mid nineteenth century and historically popular in England. The not unnatural assumption has tended to be that it was named to capitalise on the appeal of the satirical magazine launched at around the same time. Not so, says cigar professor Min Ron Nee, who believes that it was the wife-beating puppet who inspired the marque. 'The brand was very likely named after the character Mr Punch of a very popular puppet show in the UK. Mr Punch still appears on the vista of Punch Semi Plain Boxes today,' says Nee. 'Many people say that the name came from the famous British comic magazine *Punch*. This was rather unlikely, as the *Punch* magazine was established in 1841, one year after the registration of the Punch brand.'[3]

STRENGTH: Medium

FLAVOUR: Woody and complex

CHARACTER: Balanced

BEST ENJOYED: As a Double Corona

Whatever the origin of the name, the brand was a success and with its stablemates Hoyo de Monterrey, Belinda and L'Escepcion accounted for 13 per cent of Havana cigar exports in 1958. Hoyo and Punch share a home in the La Corona factory to this day. Punch is a solid medium to occasionally fuller-bodied cigar.

The Punch Punch (so good they named it twice) is a classic Corona Gorda that delivers plenty of flavour. However, to my taste the Double Corona is one of the greats in this format. Almost as much of a legend as its Hoyo counterpart, it ages sensationally well and is a couple of hours well spent. However, if you do not have the time at your disposal, follow the example of noted cigar connoisseur Sir David Tang, who imports Havana cigars into Asia and set a

[3] Min Ron Nee, *An Illustrated Encyclopaedia of Post-Revolution Havana Cigars* (Interpro Business Corp, Hong Kong, 2003), p.326

trend for the sawn-off Punch Double Corona, chopping it in half to create, in effect, two short Robustos.

⟨ QUINTERO ⟩

The best that can be said of this brand of short filler cigars is that it is affordable.

STRENGTH: Medium

FLAVOUR: Not the most refined

CHARACTER: Cheap and moderately cheerful

BEST ENJOYED: On a tight budget

⟨ RAFAEL GONZÁLEZ ⟩

These refined cigars achieve mildness while avoiding blandness. I have an emotional attachment to the light and delicate flavours of Rafael González – I was particularly partial to the Corona Extra as a youngster and still remember with pleasure one that I enjoyed in 1991 after lunch at the Colombe d'Or in Saint-Paul-de-Vence. While it is not the strongest of cigars, it is pretty powerful when it comes to making lasting memories.

The brand is believed to date from the 1920s or 1930s, and each box carries the splendidly vague legend:

These cigars have been manufactured from a secret blend of pure Vuelta Abajo tobaccos selected by the Marquez Rafael González, Grandee of Spain. For more than 20 years this brand has existed. In order that the Connoisseur may fully appreciate the perfect fragrance they should be smoked either within one month of the date of shipment from Havana or should be carefully matured for about one year.

Quite how much of this elegantly scripted nonsense is true is debatable; I seem to remember hearing that it was cooked up by an early-twentieth-century cigar merchant visiting Havana who wanted a new brand and was written out on the spot by someone who had a neat hand.

Whatever the origin, my fondness for Rafael González was compounded when I used to eat lunch at Mark's Club. As soon as my pudding had been cleared away, the inimitable Costa would be at my side proffering a Rafael González Lonsdale: it is said that Rafael González was the first brand to name a cigar Lonsdale (the *vitola de galera* is Cervantes), and the box that Costa would bring to the table had a picture of the famous sporting earl on the inside of the lid; they were special stock from the seventies, and even though I only got round to them in the 1990s, they were a delight.

STRENGTH: Light

FLAVOUR: Wafts above its weight

CHARACTER: Fragrant

BEST ENJOYED: Mid-afternoon with a cup of Lapsang Souchong

⟨ RAMÓN ALLONES ⟩

A brand of which I am wary as on occasion it is too powerful for me, demonstrating a combination of the steamroller strength of Bolívar and the spiciness of Partagás. Another characteristic it shares with Partagás is that it was founded by an ambitious and resourceful Spanish émigré eponym, one of the most innovative cigar magnates of the nineteenth century.

My wariness notwithstanding, Ramón Allones is a hugely important Havana brand. Founded in 1837, it is credited with being the first brand to use colour lithography to decorate its boxes and differentiate them from competitors, a notion that rapidly became an inalienable aspect of the cigar experience. It is also said to have been the first to adopt the triple-decker 8-9-8 way of packing cigars, which, as the numbers suggest, involves a layer of eight cigars, then a layer of nine, and a further top layer of eight.

Sometimes attaining Bolívar levels of strength, the Ramón Allones marque is particularly appreciated in the United Kingdom, where its power and flavour are enjoyed by those who enjoy country pursuits such as fishing and shooting. A robust cigar is required for al fresco enjoyment in climatic conditions that are not always forgiving and that bear little resemblance to those of Havana.

Specially Selected is a Robusto by name and nature, while the Double Corona is called Gigantes, a name that says it all. Not to be tackled by the neophyte or those of nervous disposition, it requires a strong constitution and a seasoned palate.

STRENGTH: Strong to overpowering

FLAVOUR: Power-packed, manly, fiery agreeably sour

CHARACTER: Muscular

BEST ENJOYED: On the final drive of the day after a stout shooting lunch

⟨ *ROMEO y JULIETA* ⟩

Havana may be a long way from Verona, but the story of the doomed lovers of Shakespeare's most famous tragedy took root in the fertile soil of Cuba and gave birth to one of its most versatile and appealing brands.

Though Romeo y Julieta is commonly believed to have been founded in the 1870s, cigar sleuth Min Ron Nee has traced its origins back to the 1850s. However, whatever the date of its foundation, the brand can really be said to have taken off in 1903, when it was bought by an enthusiastic and downright colourful plutocrat called Don 'Pepin' Rodriguez, whose talent for promotion was as limitless as his funds. Upon acquiring the brand, one of his first PR ploys was to try 'to buy the Capulet Hotel in Verona, as befitted the brand name. After lengthy discussions and protracted transactions, Pepin Rodriguez succeeded in obtaining the concession for a tobacconist's shop in the hotel foyer, but on one condition – each

new foreign visitor would be presented with a cigar.'[4] He also made use of Bock's invention of the cigar band like no one else before him; at one point during his stewardship of the marque, no fewer 'than 20,000 different bands were used in the production of cigars'.[5] From Gonzalez Byass to the Cienfuegos Yacht Club: if you wanted a personalised band wrapped around your cigar, then Romeo y Julieta would be happy to oblige.

Further PR came in the ample shape of British wartime leader Winston Churchill, who is said to have admired the brand. 'Following his visit to Havana in 1946, his name has not only been commemorated on a band, but it has also served to describe the marque's most famous size – Romeo y Julieta Churchills.'[6] Properly kept, a Romeo y Julieta Churchill can improve for decades.

However, it was not until the twenty-first century that the patronage of the greatest Briton and the world's most famous cigar smoker was further exploited with the arrival of the Robusto-sized Short Churchill in 2006 (a long-overdue Robusto Romeo); four years later, the Wide (55 ring gauge)

[4]   Bernard Le Roy and Maurice Szafran, *The Illustrated History of Cigars* (Harold Starke Publishing, 1998), p.58

[5]   Mark Brutton, *The World of the Habano* (Habanos, 2012), p.84

[6]   Ibid.

B
R
A
N
D
S

Churchill (really a wide Robusto) was launched; and in 2012 the Petit Churchill (a 50 × 4 in/102 mm sawn-off Robusto) came along. All are rather good cigars: easy, dependable, fruity and spicy without being overpowering – their popularity with occasional cigar smokers is testified to by the wide range of tubed Romeo y Julietas.

Aside from a full range with ring gauges from 30 to 55, the brand has plenty of eccentricities. There is the Cazadores (Hunter), which comes wrapped in silver paper and has the pungent, earthy character that might find favour with the rugged outdoorsman but not with me. More to my liking is the trio of 42 ring gauge cigars in varying lengths known as the Cedros Deluxe (Nos. 1, 2 and 3), each wrapped in a small sheet of cedar wood to add a little extra elegance and aroma.

STRENGTH: Medium

FLAVOUR: Packed with it

CHARACTER: Versatile and approachable

BEST ENJOYED: Such is the range that there is almost always a Romeo y Julieta suitable for the occasion, whatever it is

⟨ *SANCHO PANZA* ⟩

A hidden gem among Havanas, the long-suffering supporting actor of *Don Quixote* finally got top billing in 1848 when his name was given to a cigar brand. The memory of Don Quixote's squire is done justice with these excellent cigars.

Sancho Panza is a grand example of why being unfashionable can be a very good thing indeed. As it is not a trendy brand, the blend has been left alone. Moreover, the line-up has not been expanded, thus the sizes are classic: Lonsdale, Petit Corona and Belicoso, the last a medium-strength Torpedo with real distinction.

Entertainingly, the Lonsdale's factory name is Cervantes and the name it is given in the Sancho Panza brand is Molino (Windmill). But the star of the line-up, when you can find it, is the Sancho Panza Sanchos. The same size as the Montecristo A, 9¼ in/235 mm in length, this is a fine and mellow cigar, or at least the ones I have are, because they have been knocking around since the mid-1990s. The passage of time has removed any sharper edges, making it well worth the effort it takes to find them.

STRENGTH: Medium

FLAVOUR: Well structured with some body but not overpowering

CHARACTER: As reliable as their eponym

BEST ENJOYED: While tilting at windmills

⦓ SAN CRISTÓBAL de la HABANA ⦔

This is an underrated brand making some excellent cigars that take their names from the fortresses that defended the city when it was the pearl of Spain's colonial possessions.

I remember being particularly taken with this brand of lighter- to medium-bodied cigars when they launched in 1999. At that time the line-up featured El Morro (49 × 7 in/178 mm), sadly now out of production; La Fuerza (50 × 5½ in/140 mm); La Punta (52 × 5½ in/140 mm); and El Principe (42 × 4⅜ in/110 mm). The cigars tend to be of medium strength, and given that they are often overlooked, they usually have a bit of age on them.

For a number of years I was very partial to La Fuerza, a *vitola* known as a Gordito; it was one of the very first long Robustos. It was delicious in a medium-bodied sort of way, but then as cigars became ever more generously proportioned, I rather lost sight of it among the forest of sequoia-sized smokes heading out of the factories of Havana. However, the real star of the brand is the pint-sized Principe, which is a brilliantly versatile cigar, elegant enough for the first coffee on a summer's morning and yet with just sufficient flavour to justify post-prandial use.

Subsequent to their appearance at the end of the last century, there have been a number of special editions of San Cristóbal carrying an inevitable second claret-coloured band indicating that they were once only available in Casas del Habano (the global network of Havana-only cigar stores). These tend to be a little girthier, richer and spicier than the original range, but have yielded some real gems, including the Torreon (54 × 6 in/152 mm), housed in a highly idiosyncratic porcelain jar, with a lid bearing fortress-like crenellations that also serves as an ashtray (the appearance is of a gaudy rook from an oversized chess set). The preposterous packaging conceals a cigar well worth seeking out, as whoever put it together clearly knew what they were doing.

It begins with a dry flavour and roast coffee bean aroma, and it is the flavour rather than the strength that develops. Early dried fruit flavours lead to a pleasing and lively spiciness, and the smoke is that perfect silvered blue.

San Cristóbal is not a widely appreciated marque, a state of affairs I hope will continue.

STRENGTH: Medium

FLAVOUR: Woody with various degrees of spice

CHARACTER: Mature

BEST ENJOYED: After lunch or a light supper

⟨ TRINIDAD ⟩

For years this cigar enjoyed almost mythical status. El Commandante's favourite diplomatic gift, the Cohiba, came onto the market in the early 1980s; while the Trinidad, although inaugurated a couple of years after the Cohiba in 1969,[7] retained its air of myth and mystery until well into the 1990s. It was not until Marvin R. Shanken's modest little supper party in 1994 in Paris, a $1,000-a-head cigar dinner nicknamed 'Dinner of the Century', that the existence of these cigars was proved beyond doubt. It was a major

[7] Adriano Martínez Rius, cited in Nee, *An Illustrated Encyclopaedia*, p.472

Arranging the contents of a box of cigars in order of colour in the Trinidad factory

moment in cigar history; imagine the Yeti being captured or the Loch Ness monster appearing in an aquarium.

It was still such a novelty a couple of years later that I remember attending a cigar dinner in about 1996 when one of the guests actually turned down a Trinidad, saying rather loftily that he only smoked Cuban cigars; he clearly believed these to be a product of the island of Trinidad, when in fact the name is derived from the Cuban city, a UNESCO heritage site and a favourite with visitors to the island on account of its colonial architecture.

Originally available only as a single size – the long (7½ in/192 mm), slender (38 ring gauge) Lanceros, complete with pigtail head – even the blend was similar to Cohiba, albeit without the additional fermentation. When it was made commercially available in 1998, in strictly limited quantities, the ring gauge was increased slightly to 40, a *vitola* known as the Laguito Especial, given the Trinidad name of Fundador, and boasted a blend devised by the legendary Raoul Valladares of El Laguito. It remained a single-size brand until 2003, when three further cigars were added to the range: the Robusto Extra (50 × 6⅛ in/156 mm); the Coloniales (44 × 5¼ in/132 mm); and the Reyes (40 × 4⅜ in/110 mm), again equipped with the pigtail head.

I remember visiting the Laguito factory, where all Trinidads were made at that time, and getting very excited about the Robusto Extra. Sure enough, along with its two new siblings, it proved so popular that Trinidad outgrew El Laguito and production was transferred to Pinar del Río. I remember one slightly embarrassing visit to the factory there, when I was given a cigar from which I kept pulling twig-like bits of stalk until it drew properly. However, occasional cavils about quality aside, the cigars were delicious, light to medium in strength, but rounded and almost sweet; they age well.

With the introduction of the Robusto T in 2009 – a delicious cigar that one aficionado of my acquaintance told me was good enough to eat, let alone smoke – the brand seemed to have established itself firmly on the market and in the humidors of connoisseurs. So it should not have come as a surprise that in 2012 the Robusto T and Robusto Extra (in my view the stars of the range) were withdrawn; if you are fortunate enough to come across a box of either, do not hesitate to snap them up.

For a while there was uncertainty about Trinidad's prospects, but with the 2014 launch of the Vigia (54 × 4³⁄₈ in/110 mm), a bulked-up, on-trend sawn-off Robusto offering a fuller, stronger and spicier take, it would seem that the brand has a future.

STRENGTH: Medium

FLAVOUR: Traditionally mellow but getting livelier

CHARACTER: Diplomatic

BEST ENJOYED: During the day, wasted after a heavy dinner

⟨ *VEGAS ROBAINA* ⟩

During the 1990s, one man emerged as the 'face' of Cuba's cigar industry: a face that would have given the pachydermally creased and fissured features of W. H. Auden a run for their money. Alejandro Robaina was a hero of the revolution. During the Batista years he carried on cultivating tobacco while concealing rebels on his farm (including Fernández Roig, official eponym of the Partagás factory) and collecting money for the guerrillas. 'I continued, as always, on the plantations, seeing to my harvest. In that very same tobacco house where I dried my tobacco harvest of 1959, I had fourteen men hidden there, men that were in the Revolution,'[8] he would later recall.

Three decades on, he became a hero of the cigar industry, managing to produce high-quality wrapper leaf during the difficult 1989 harvest. His yield of usable leaf was known to top an impressive 80 per cent, and by the mid-1990s this considerable achievement was recognised with an award naming him Cuba's best tobacco farmer, presented by Fidel Castro in person. In one of his worst years he managed a yield of only 36 per cent, but to put that into context, some of the state farms that year only achieved 0·8 per cent.[9]

Farming land that had been cultivated by his family since 1845, Alejandro embarked on his working life as a child. If one regards one's first cigar as an act of maturity, he came of age at 10 years old, when he ignited his first home-grown and rolled cigar. In 1951, at the age of 32, he took over the running of the plantation on the death of his father, and built on its reputation for fine wrapper leaves, spending the rest of his life perfecting his art. Such was the

[8]   J. L. Milán, *Alejandro Robaina, Tradition and Magnanimity* (Epicur Publicaciones SL, 2004), p.5

[9]   James Suckling, 'Cigar Diary: Cuba's Cigar Legend', *Cigar Aficionado* website, posted 1 October 2006

B
R
A
N
D
S

quality of his wrappers that the Cuban government selected them for use on the original Trinidad cigars that were given as diplomatic gifts.

It was only well into his seventies that he became, in cigar terms, a rock star. The cigar boom taught a new generation to love the tobacco of the Vuelta Abajo, and the appeal of Cuba's cigars – their link with the *terroir*, their authenticity and their tradition –seemed to be summed up in Alejandro Robaina. He was honoured, as Davidoff had been before him, with an eponymous cigar; not one that he had made himself, but one that carried his picture. If anything, in style and delivery of flavour they can be described as having some similarities to the Montecristo range, but with a fuller, stronger, earthier taste.

Over the years, this unlikely pin-up of the industry became a globe-trotting ambassador. Nor did he get much respite when he returned to Cuba. His farm was a place of pilgrimage, with cigar fans desperate to catch a glimpse of, and share a few moments with, their idol. I have to admit that I was one of the groupies who made their way out to the plantation at Cuchillas de Barbacoa (literally 'ridges of the barbecue'). My recollection of him from a day spent primarily in rocking chairs smoking the home-rolled cigars that had sustained him since his tenth birthday is of a gentle and unassuming man, who talked much about the rhythms of the seasons and the changes in climate that he had noticed over the course of his long career in tobacco.

Of course Robaina, with his straw hat and sun-fissured features, embodied the ideal image of the tobacco farmer; but he also showed that when it comes to making cigars, men of character are just as important as tobacco leaves.

Alejandro Robaina on his farm at Pinar del Rio, Vuelta Abajo

The cigars that bear his name are like a punchy Montecristo or a less aggressive Ramón Allones with a sprinkling of spiciness. The standard range is compact, just five *vitolas*, the stars of which are the Famoso (a near Robusto) and the Unico (Pirámide). A recent Famoso with a beautiful glossy chestnut-coloured wrapper smelt wonderful even unlit – honeyed and pickled all at once. About half an inch in, it settled down to a woody, tangy, agreeably vegetal flavour that was lively enough to maintain interest and was delivered firmly but not overpoweringly to the palate. Not the most refined or elegant of blends, but, as a celebration of a man who made his life out of the Cuban soil, rather fitting.

STRENGTH: Full

FLAVOUR: Spicy and earthy

CHARACTER: Firm and rustic

BEST ENJOYED: In a rocking chair on your verandah after a hard day in the fields

NEW WORLD CIGARS

Although the countries of Central and South America were historically involved in the cultivation of tobacco, and in some cases the manufacture of finished cigars, the rise of modern cigar making in the region can be dated to the early 1960s. The Cuban revolution drove a great many cigar-making and tobacco-cultivating families into exile. Many settled in neighbouring countries, where the politics, climate and soil were similar to those of their pre-revolutionary homeland, and once President Kennedy imposed the trade embargo as a result of the Missile Crisis; Cuban cigars were no longer available in the United States, leaving the market open to competitor nations.

A second stimulus was given to non-Cuban manu-facturers during the 1990s, when a cigar boom gripped the United States, which, unable to acquire (legally at least) Cuban cigars, had to turn elsewhere for its supplies.

It is incorrect to say that Havana cigars are better than other cigars, but they are different. Cigars demon-strate characteristics specific to their region, their maker and their market. And the chief difference between Cuban and non-Cuban cigars is that while Havana cigars are *puros*, those made elsewhere in the region tend to draw freely on tobacco from other countries: a cigar made in the Dominican Republic may have an Ecuadorean wrapper and filler sourced from across the region as well as that grown in its own fields. Thus the palette of flavours upon which a skilful blender can draw is vast.

Although each country is capable of offering various styles of cigars, it is generally accepted that those from the Dominican Republic tend to be lighter, with a crisp saltiness, while those from Nicaragua are the most powerful and spicy. New World cigars have pioneered eye-catching packaging as extravagant and innovative as the dressed box must have appeared at the time of its introduction in the nineteenth century. Another innovation led by the New World makers has been the adoption of ever-larger ring gauges; whereas Cuba only got its first 60 ring gauge cigar in 2016, with the Cohiba 50 Aniversario, certain non-Cuban makers have been producing cigars of this girth since the early years of the twenty-first century, and sequoia-like ring gauges of up to 80 are known.

COSTA RICA

A relative newcomer to the cultivation of cigar tobacco, with topographical, climatic and geological similarities with other noted tobacco-producing countries in the region. Costa Rica benefits from rich volcanic soil and the cloud cover that means wrapper can be cultivated with no need to place it under cloth.

For almost 150 miles the Cibao valley runs like a vast trench across the north of the country, from Manzanilla Bay close to the border with Haiti in the west to Samana in the east. It is bounded to the north by the Septentrional mountains and to the south by the dramatic crags of the Central range, with the Caribbean's highest mountain, Pico Duarte. On the valley floor are rice paddies; in the mountains coffee is grown; and in between, tobacco is planted. During the second half of the nineteenth century much of its tobacco industry was controlled by Germany, establishing a bond between German-speaking countries and Dominican tobacco that endures to this day (Davidoff is headquartered in the Swiss-German city of Basel).

While leaf tobacco was exported to make cigars in Europe, nineteenth-century domestic consumption was characterised by the Andullo, a tightly bound covering of palm leaves around a length of tobacco so compressed as to become a block that could be transported to market and cut in lengths for sale. (The Andullo is still made today and enjoys considerable popularity with Dominican expatriates in the USA.) The local economy began to improve with the sugar cane boom of the 1880s, and small cigar factories began to appear: first was Matilde in the 1880s, then in 1901 La Habanera, followed in 1903 by the famous La Aurora.

After the end of the First World War and the collapse of Germany as an imperialist colonial power, the Dutch, a nationality with historic ties to the tobacco industry, took a leading role; among them was Henke Kelner's family, who settled in Santiago in 1925. Unlike its Central American neighbours, the Dominican Republic did not benefit immediately from the exodus of tobacco and cigar expertise from Cuba in the wake of the revolution, as it was far from politically stable itself. In May 1961, the country's leader, another prototypical Latin American dictator, Rafael Leónidas Trujillo, was ambushed on a coast road and gunned down by a party of conspirators. An attempt by his son Ramfis to succeed him ended with the flight of the entire Trujillo family later that year. It was only after an American invasion in 1965 ended an incipient civil war and backed the robustly anti-communist rule of Joaquín Balaguer, under whose administration the first duty-free zones were established, that the country became attractive to large international companies and smaller makers fleeing instability elsewhere in the region.

Today in terms of output the fertile furrow of the Cibao valley is the heart of the cigar industry, not just in the Dominican Republic but in the region as a whole, with an estimated annual production of 210 million hand-made cigars. Second place is occupied by Nicaragua with 135 million, then Cuba with 85 million, just ahead of Honduras with 75 million. The country is home to some of the biggest and best-known brands, among them Davidoff and Fuente. During the nineteenth century the city of Santiago de los Caballeros in the middle of the valley was more populous than the capital, Santo Domingo, with as much as 70 per cent of the population living in the area. It may be the country's second city, but it is its cigar capital and is fiercely proud of its traditions, among them cockfighting.

ECUADOR

Known in particular for wrapper leaves, the Los Ríos province of Ecuador in the Andean foothills, inland from the city of Guayaquil, benefits from an interesting microclimate where nearly constant cloud coverage creates the perfect conditions for wrapper leaf without having to resort to the technique of shade growing under cloth. Moreover, dozens of active volcanoes provide a nutrient-rich soil. Connecticut seed that yields light toffee-coloured wrappers, Sumatra seed to make darker and oilier wrappers, and various Habano seed varieties are planted here.

The best-known growers in Ecuador are the Perez family, who supply top-quality makers across the region. The dynasty originated in Cuba, inevitably, where José Perez grew tobacco from the 1880s. After the revolution, his grandson Silvio left for Miami. During the 1960s, Silvio and his son Alfredo worked for the Cullman family, owners of General Cigar, superintending wrapper production in Connecticut. After a Nicaraguan wrapper-growing experiment, their purchase of an Ecuadorean farm in 1991 was perfectly timed to benefit from the cigar boom, and the business is now run by David and Joseph Perez.

HONDURAS

Filler is still grown in Copán, the original tobacco cultivation area of Honduras, where the Spanish government set up a branch of its Real Fábrica de Tabacos in the eighteenth century, and there is a local wild strain of tobacco called Copecan. However, today the cigar capital is Danlí, and the Jamastran valley, a source of filler and wrapper, is seen as the Pinar del Río of Honduras. Given its proximity to the border with Nicaragua, the tobacco grown here shares characteristics of strength and richness with that cultivated by its southern neighbour. North-east of Danlí is the Olancho region, another source of filler and wrapper as well as the location of many clandestine airstrips used by drug runners, which have given the region an unwelcome reputation as the most violent part of the country. The Talanga valley, some of which is planted with Corojo, is celebrated for its wrappers.

MEXICO

The San Andrés valley in Mexico's Veracruz state is the centre of tobacco cultivation. And although like other countries in the region there is historical evidence of tobacco growing, the

cigar industry in this large, populous nation is some way behind that of its southern neighbours in Central America. Local industry remains largely focused on the domestic market: in 2015, Mexico exported only around five million cigars, and until recently, legislation and high tariffs militated against the import of tobacco leaves from other nations, which restricted variety. Tabacalera Alberto Turrent, established in 1880, is the largest producer, maker of Mexico's most famous brand, Te-Amo, and also a significant grower of three types of tobacco: Sumatra (for wrappers), Habano Criollo and San Andrés Negro.

NICARAGUA

Cigar making in Nicaragua centres on the city of Estelí, to the north of which are the Condega valley growing region and the Jalapa valley, Nicaragua's Vuelta Abajo, where the steamy climate together with the rich soil give birth to some of the best tobacco currently being grown. Emigrés from Cuba, including the Padrón family, believed that Nicaragua offered conditions similar to Cuba and established themselves here. It was not only the soil and weather that were familiar and reassuring; the political climate was propitious, as the Somoza family which had run the country more as a family estate than a nation from the 1930s, enjoyed the backing of the United States (to the extent that Nicaragua produced the official cigars of Nixon's White House).[11]

By the 1970s, Nicaraguan tobacco had built itself a fine reputation. Anastasio Somoza, the last family member to rule the country, owned tobacco farms and appropriated the cigar company Joya de Nicaragua. However, the cigar industry was almost destroyed by the civil war, not least when the United States imposed a decade-long embargo on Nicaraguan products. Since then Nicaragua has made up for lost time and become the Klondike of the cigar world, with brands and fortunes being built with much the same rapidity as in Havana during the nineteenth century; and that is not the sole similarity with Cuba. Nicaragua is self-sufficient in

[11]   http://joyacigars.com, accessed 6 June 2016

tobacco terms: in other words, it can make *puros* just as in Cuba. Moreover, many of the varieties of seed planted are of Cuban origin.

As Nicaraguan tobacco tends to be quite forceful and spicy, it is often used by makers of cigars elsewhere to enrich and energise otherwise unexciting blends. According to Henke Kelner, sometimes Nicaraguan growers strip a tobacco plant back to just 12 leaves (as opposed to the customary 16–18) to further concentrate the nutrients in a smaller number of thicker, more powerful leaves. He also adds that on occasion the strength of the Nicaraguan cigars is compounded by a harshness that comes from incompletely fermented tobacco, a commercial short cut that has since emerged as a cherished flavour characteristic. This sense of distinct regional character has helped make Nicaragua one of the most exciting and dynamic cigar-producing countries.

⟨ ALEC BRADLEY ⟩

If you were looking for a name that tells the story of the American cigar during the 20 years from the late 1990s, you could do worse than study Alec Bradley, a brand named after the children of former hardware supplier Alan Rubin, who used the proceeds of the sale of his successful business to start in the cigar industry in the late 1990s, and as such found himself perfectly placed to enter the trough after the boom. Bad timing was compounded by even worse branding: the rather appallingly named Bogey's Stogies focused on the very tight market of cigar-smoking golfers, and were sold in golf shops under the motto 'The only bogey you'll ever enjoy on the golf course'.[2] To no one's surprise, except perhaps his own, the business was a disaster. 'I'm a Florida boy and I thought that people played golf 12 months out of the year in the entire country,' Rubin admitted to *Cigar Aficionado* in 2011, looking back on his youthful folly. 'It was kind of a faulty business plan.'[3]

By then, he was the proprietor of a successful boutique cigar brand. In 2000, many cigar makers had spare capacity; one of them was the legendary Henke Kelner, creator of the Dominican Davidoffs, who made cigars for Rubin, at Davidoff's private-label factory 'Occidental'. Alec Bradley's Occidental Reserve kept Rubin in the business, and demonstrating his flair for the novelty cigar, he also launched Trilogy, a pressed cigar with a triangular profile that appeared to have been inspired by a bar of Toblerone. His breakthrough cigar was the head-spinningly strong Tempus, made by a small Honduran factory called Raices Cubanas. Alec Bradley cigars are also made by Plasencia.

Today Alec Bradley has gone gourmet. The Nicaraguan Prensado is well regarded in America and demonstrates the slightly raw but nonetheless chocolatey and peppery characteristics of Nicaraguan cigars. There is also a following for the Fine and Rare series, whose cigars carry not so much a

[2]   http://www.cigaraficionado.com/webfeatures/show/id/15886, accessed 7 June 2016

[3]   Ibid.

ALEC BRADLEY

band as a scroll detailing their date of rolling, date of release, weekly production, length, ring gauge, and names and signatures of roller, supervisor and the men who approved it. Cigars in this series tend to be complex and carefully studied – quite a journey from Bogey's Stogies. Happily, the brand has not lost its knack for silly names or novelty cigars, combining the two in the Black Market Filthy Hooligan, a blend of Honduran, Nicaraguan and Panamanian tobacco characterised by its unique barber's-pole wrapper that alternates Oscuro with light green Candela.

STRENGTH: Can be substantial

FLAVOUR: Expect punchy notes of Nicaraguan tobacco

CHARACTER: All-American

BEST ENJOYED: On the golf course in honour of the original Bogey's Stogie

⟨ *ARTURO FUENTE* ⟩

Among the first wave of Cuban emigrés who left the island at the beginning of the twentieth century following the devastating Spanish–American war was 14-year-old Arturo Fuente; ten years later, in 1912, he opened an eponymous cigar business in West Tampa, one of many dozen cigar-making factories importing Cuban tobacco and producing cigars. Fuente prospered, and by 1924 he employed 500 people. However, a disastrous fire destroyed his factory building and it was not until the Great Depression and the Second World War had passed that he resumed production, and then only on a very local basis, installing a few rolling tables on his back porch.

A year before the Cuban revolution, Arturo's son Carlos Fuente took over and the fortunes of the family turned. With the US embargo in place, Carlos started buying tobacco from Puerto Rico and Colombia, experimenting with blends that would appeal to palates accustomed to Cuban leaf. The company prospered, and during the 1970s Carlos moved production to Estelí, but the decade ended badly when, 55 years after the Tampa building had been destroyed by fire, the Fuente factory was burned to the ground during the Nicaraguan revolution.

Mortgaging his house and scraping together what funds he could find, Carlos set out for the Dominican Republic, and in September 1980 Tabacalera A. Fuente opened a 12,000-square-foot factory in Santiago. With the launch in 1980 of the medium-bodied Hemingway line, the family re-established its reputation.

At the end of the 1980s, the company began to grow tobacco on a substantial scale and took on the challenge of developing its own wrapper leaf. The result of this period of investment and development can be tasted in the Fuente Opus X range, introduced in 1995 and characterised by the pinkish 'Rosado' wrapper. One of the first of the so-called power cigars to grab the attention of the American market (in the early 1990s most cigars sold in the US were mild, with pale wrappers), it became a cult during the cigar boom, with scarcity and high pricing only heightening the frenzy. It is now an established classic, with strong, fruity flavours. I recently enjoyed an old Opus X that I had kept in my humidor for some years, and I can only describe the feeling as like being knocked out by a large, rich Dundee cake: the cigar was undeniably extremely well constructed and equally undeniably powerful, with a wall of rich flavours including nuts and dried fruit.

In 2010, Carlos Fuente and his son, Carlos Fuente Jr, produced 30 million cigars, and the Fuente fan base supports a range of other products, including a partnership with the Hublot watch brand.

STRENGTH: Punchy

FLAVOUR: Spicy, fruity, nutty

CHARACTER: Sophisticated yet strong

BEST ENJOYED: When you are rested, well fed and not intending to operate heavy machinery

⟨ AVO ⟩

Nonagenarian Avo Uvezian is an enigmatic character of Armenian descent and extravagant manner who dresses as does the man from Del Monte. In his dazzling white suit and broad-brimmed straw hat he would have looked entirely in keeping with the belle époque crowd in Monte Carlo, but it was in Puerto Rico that he segued from a career in music to a second life as a cigar brand. After a picaresque and peripatetic career as a musician that had taken him from the Lebanon to the US via Damascus, Baghdad and the court of the Shah of Iran, he moved to Puerto Rico in 1971. Here he established himself as a piano player at the Palmas del Mar resort, dabbled in real estate and added cigar making to what today would be called a portfolio career.

He used to have a few cigars made for him, which he sold singly from a jar atop his piano. After a couple of years his cigars became so popular that he began selling them in boxes. By the 1980s, demand was such that he went to see Henke Kelner and his master blender Eladio Diaz in Santiago de los Caballeros in the Dominican Republic, where Henke had recently opened a small factory with six rollers making private label cigars. At the fuller-flavoured end of the Dominican range, Avo's cigars acquired such a following that he sent a batch to the then recently opened Davidoff store in New York: 125,000 were sold in the first year, and soon it became several hundred thousand per year. Now the Avo brand is owned by Oettinger Davidoff and made in the Oettinger Kelner factory located next to the Davidoff factory near Santiago.

Typically, Avo cigars have tended to be made with Dominican filler and binder, often well aged, with Ecuadorean wrappers grown from Connecticut or Cuban/Connecticut hybrid seeds. Recently, however, the marque has been exploring the possibilities offered by other Central American countries; for instance the Avo limited edition released for his birthday in March 2016 and housed in a box that looks like a record player features an Ecuadorean wrapper grown from Habano 2000 seed, and Mexican

Negro San Andrés with the Dominican filler. In line with the current interest in Nicaraguan tobacco, the Avo Syncro Nicaragua is a cigar with dark and oily Ecuadorean wrapper, and binder and filler from the Dominican Republic, Peru and the Nicaraguan island of Ometepe. The intense, peppery Nicaraguan tobacco is tempered by the creamy and aromatic Dominican leaves.

STRENGTH: Medium

FLAVOUR: Smooth, creamy

CHARACTER: Musical

BEST ENJOYED: With friends while wearing a white suit and playing the piano

⟨ *CAMACHO* ⟩

A brand that should really drop the first two letters of its name, Camacho, founded by Cuban émigré Simon Camacho, is now owned by Oettinger Davidoff. Based in Danlí in Honduras, it is most famous for its use of what it calls 'Original Corojo' – except of course that the original Corojo was grown on the Corojo plantation in Cuba. 'Loud' and 'unapologetic' are the technical terms that best describe Camacho cigars. Typical is the Camacho Custom Built series, apparently what the 'Big Dogs' smoke, among them a Hall of Fame American football player and coach called Mike Ditka. Other gems include the Camacho Powerband, supposedly 'inspired by the power, performance and acceleration of the classic V-twin engine'.[4]

One of Camacho's greatest hits is the American Barrel Aged line, which is made with filler aged for five months in American bourbon barrels; an intriguing concept that has taken off like one of the muscle cars that I am sure every Camacho smoker drives. The Brotherhood series is 'a celebration of the bond between men who take action and never sit idly by'.[5] The copywriting may at times collapse into parody-defying hyperbole, but the cigars are not at all bad. Unlit, the basic Camacho Corojo has a lovely bouquet akin to that of a freshly opened bag of raisins; it is strong and to my palate a little harsh – an assessment that no doubt marks me out as insufficiently manly to pursue what Camacho proudly calls 'The Loud Life' and which I imagine is lived at full volume.

STRENGTH: Can be that of a champion arm wrestler

FLAVOUR: Rich and raisin-like

CHARACTER: In your face

BEST ENJOYED: While doing something manly

[4] http://camachocigars.com/cigars, accessed 3 July 2016

[5] http://www.cigaraficionado.com/webfeatures/show/id/15886, accessed 7 June 2016

‹ *DAVIDOFF* ›

When Davidoff announced that it was moving its production from Cuba to the Dominican Republic, it was as if the respected Swiss marque had detonated a bomb. The cigar world went into shock. Zino Davidoff had first gone to Cuba in the 1920s. His counsel and his patronage had been sought by makers of Havana cigars before and after the revolution. During the years after the war he invented the Chateau series of cigars named after the great wines of Bordeaux. And he had been accorded the ultimate acclaim of having a cigar brand named in his honour. His name had become a synonym for the very best that the fields of the Vuelta Abajo could grow and the *torcedores* of Havana could roll ... and now, after a lifetime together, the two were parting. A mix of concerns about quality and the future of the brand if it remained in Cuba prompted Ernst Schneider, the shrewd leader of Oettinger Davidoff, as the company became known in 1970, to seek an alternative, and he placed the future of the Davidoff marque in the hands of a remarkable man.

Cigar Aficionado magazine has likened him to such towering gastronomic talents as Alain Ducasse and Joel Robuchon, and the comparison is an apt one, as Henke Kelner conjures a seemingly limitless range of flavours and aromas from his raw materials. The comparison with great chefs is particularly appropriate, as Henke believes in 'total palate stimulation', which he achieves by blending a range of leaves: different varieties of tobacco, cultivated in different soils and different countries, taken from different positions on the plant.

It is a message that his key staff have learnt well. Instead of talking in vague flavour similes of leather, wood and so on (I cannot remember the last time I ate any leather, and aside from chewing pencils in school, my experiences of wood flavours is limited), when offering a cigar they ask what sort of palate stimulation one is seeking. (Another linguistic quirk of the Davidoff approach is that one is asked whether one would like to enjoy rather than smoke a cigar.) In addition, it is hard to imagine a more exactly made and dependable cigar. 'All that we do in our factories, all that our 1,300 people do, is only for the satisfaction of the cigar smoker. That is the goal,' says Henke[61].

Oettinger Davidoff manufactures somewhere in the region of 46 million cigars annually, more than some countries and more than half of the entire output of hand-made long-filler cigars from Cuba. The enormity of this achievement is even more impressive for those who have seen the factory in which it all started, little more than a barn with a stamped-earth floor.

Classic

Subtle and light, these slender ring gauge cigars pay homage to the original Cuban-made cigars to bear the Davidoff name, made with a light traditional blend of the classic tobaccos of the Dominican Republic: Olor, Piloto and San Vicente.

Escurio

The clue is in the last three letters of the name. With their

---

[61]   Hendrik Kelner, interview with the author, June 2016

beautiful wrappers the colour of chocolate (maybe the colour suggested as much, but there is also a chocolatey hint to the cigar as it develops), and their black and silver banding, these sweet and spicy cigars are intended to evoke the spirit of a night in Rio de Janeiro. Having never been to Brazil, I am alas unable to confirm or deny that they achieve their stated aim; they are, however, intriguing cigars with a relatively approachable strength level, using dark Brazilian Mata Fina, Ecuadorean Habano seed wrapper and Cubra leaf, described by Davidoff as the fire of the Cuban Criollo refined; indeed, it is the refinement that is characteristically Davidoff. Sizes suit the modern trends and include a Gran Toro (58 ×5½ in/140 mm) and an espresso-like Petit Robusto (a sawn-off 50 ×3¼ in/83 mm).

Grand Cru

Numbered from 1 to 5, this range of relatively slender (the biggest is 43) classic ring gauges is an aromatic and slightly nutty cigar that is true to the lightness that Davidoff was aiming at when it launched its cigars from the Dominican Republic.

Millennium

As the name suggests, this line made its debut at around the turn of the century. It represents an evolution of the Special blend, with slightly bolder flavours, while still maintaining the Davidoff commitment to all-round palate stimulation.

Davidoff Millennium Toro

Nicaragua

Perhaps the most emblematic Davidoff cigar of the contemporary period, with the traditionally strong – dare one say harsh? – character of the Nicaraguan tobacco given the Davidoff touch. Imagine Tarzan leaving the jungle and swapping his loincloth for a dinner jacket: this cigar has enough of the strength, vitality, pepper, spice and fieriness you expect from a Nicaraguan cigar, and what Henke calls 'linear' stimulation tobacco; but is improved by a pleasingly civilised flavour delivery. Among the strongest of Davidoff cigars, it has caught the imagination of the cigar-smoking (sorry – cigar-enjoying) public. The box-pressed Nicaraguan is a joy and deservedly popular.

Special

This light yet satisfying blend was an early launch by Davidoff at the beginning of the Dominican years, and for the neophyte or occasional cigar smoker, something like the robusto-sized Special R is a good starting point. The range is predicated on classic sizes, including among others Double Corona, Perfecto and Culebras. Although it has since been joined by plenty of new lines, when it launched, the Special series was a revelation to me, combining excellent construction, light style and a slightly tangy, piquant flavour.

STRENGTH: Generally light to medium

FLAVOUR: Varied

CHARACTER: Civilised

BEST ENJOYED: When you have time that needs to be filled beautifully

Winston Churchill

Working with the family of the world's most famous cigar smoker and Britain's most celebrated twentieth-century statesman, Davidoff has created a line of cigars named after the various aspects of the great man's multifaceted personality. Thus the Churchill size is called the Aristocrat and the Statesman describes the Robusto, while other traits of this historic figure celebrated in fine tobacco are the Artist (Petit Corona), the Commander (Toro), the Raconteur (Petit Panetela) and the Traveller (Belicoso).

The cigars are as complex as their eponym, with tobaccos from multiple countries of origin blended to create what has become one of the Swiss brand's best-sellers.

STRENGTH: Medium

FLAVOUR: Peppery, leathery, earthy

CHARACTER: Churchillian

BEST ENJOYED: If you are an artistocrat/statesman/commander/artist/raconteur/traveller

⟨ THE GRIFFIN'S ⟩

This stablemate of Davidoff shares the classic white band of its more famous sibling, and celebrates another Geneva landmark, the Griffin's nightclub, back in its glory years during the 1960s, 1970s and 1980s. Griffin's founder, Bernard H.

'Wheels' of 50 cigars ready for packing in the factory. Caption probably not necessary

Grobet, was seldom seen without a long cigar in his hand, and given that the club was a centre for gastronomy and good times, it seems appropriate to launch a Griffin's cigar. Recently the classic white-label line was joined by a richer, spicier blend, Griffin's Nicaragua, which as well as having darker wrappers was further distinguished by offering the fashionably girthy Toro and Gran Toro formats.

STRENGTH: Mild (classic) to medium

FLAVOUR: Nicaragua is the fuller flavour, with regionally characteristic notes of spice and pepper

CHARACTER: Nocturnal

BEST ENJOYED: After dark

⌐ *EL SEPTIMO* ⌐

Distinguished by brightly coloured opaque plastic boxes and known for using aged tobacco, El Septimo produces tree-trunk-like cigars that make Robustos seem like anorexic toothpicks. The blend packs a flavoursome punch even in the smaller sizes – the little Amarillo provides a mouthful of flavour.

Wrappers are dark and oily and flavour develops and changes throughout the life of the cigar, but the chief talking point is the price, about twice that of the corresponding Cohiba.

STRENGTH: Potent

FLAVOUR: Feisty

CHARACTER: Pricey

BEST ENJOYED: If you have a lot of money and like cigars in bright plastic boxes

❮ JOYA de NICARAGUA ❯

Established in 1968, Joya de Nicaragua (Jewel of Nicaragua), located in the country's cigar capital Estelí, is the country's first premium hand-made cigar manufacturer. It was founded by Daniel Rodriguez, former owner of Cuba's fabled Corojo plantation, who was invited to Nicaragua by cigar-loving president Anastasio Somoza. For some years he successfully cultivated fields of tobacco in Jalapa, replicating as closely as he could the tobacco with which he had grown up in Cuba. However, revolution and political instability once more interrupted his career. The Joya de Nicaragua factory was burned down and Rodriguez's tobacco fields became battlefields – disillusioned, he turned his back on cigars.

Just as exports of Havana cigars to the USA were interrupted by the 35th President of the United States, so the 40th President, Ronald Reagan, imposed an embargo on Nicaraguan products, causing production of Joya de Nicaragua to move across the border to Honduras, where manufacture was continued at the Nestor Plasencia factory. Trademark difficulties added to the company's woes, but in 1994 the brand was purchased and revived by Dr Alejandro Ernesto Martínez Cuenca, who served as Minister of Foreign Trade for the

Sandinista government. The spicy Joya de Nicaragua Antaño 1970 restored the lustre of its reputation, and in recent years it has won plaudits for its Cuatro Cinco Reserve.

STRENGTH: Medium to strong

FLAVOUR: Woody and fruity

CHARACTER: Accomplished

BEST ENJOYED: If you like the taste of Nicaraguan history

⟨ *PADRÓN* ⟩

One of the legends of the non-Havana cigar world, and famous for the dark wrappers and box-pressed profile of its exquisitely made Nicaraguan cigars, the brand has an exciting rags-to-riches story. José Orlando Padrón, the scion of a poor but established tobacco-farming family from Piloto in Cuba, had joined the revolution, but soon grew disillusioned and left the island, going first to Spain and then America. He settled in Florida, where he found the quality of locally available, affordable cigars execrable, and in 1964 he set up a small factory making cigars for poor Cuban exiles using leaf from Brazil, Puerto Rico and Connecticut. In 1967, he made his first cigars using Nicaraguan tobacco, and by 1970 he had opened a factory in the Central American country.

During the seventies, his Miami headquarters was bombed by hard-line right-wing Cubans after Padrón was photographed giving Fidel Castro a cigar during negotiations for the successful release of political prisoners from Cuban jails. Meanwhile, the troubles in Nicaragua hurt his business too: in May 1978, his factory in Estelí was burned down and the war forced him to relocate to a small factory across the border in Danlí, Honduras, dark days during which a plot to kidnap him was uncovered. He did not return to Nicaragua until 1990. In 1994, the brand hit the jackpot with the launch of the Padrón 1964 Anniversary series, a line that reintroduced the box-pressed shape and established a visual identity for the marque. The Family Reserve series is the top-of-the-range Padrón, made with tobacco that has been maturing for anything up to a decade.

STRENGTH: Can sometimes make a strong Havana seem docile

FLAVOUR: Rich with pronounced sweetness

CHARACTER: Mature

BEST ENJOYED: If you like dark wrappers

⟨ TATUAJE ⟩

Spanish for 'tattoo', Tatuaje is the creation of Pete Johnson, a failed bass guitarist turned cigar success story, whose heavily tattooed arms betray the origins of his brand name and that of his nickname in the industry, 'Tattoo Pete'. His appearance is pure Quentin Tarantino, as is his route into the cigar industry, as he told *Cigar Aficionado* magazine in 2012. 'I was working as a bouncer in a strip club. I had no money. I was shopping at Gus's Smoke Shop. I loved the whole feel of the industry and I really loved cigars. This guy named Dennis Spike recommended me [to owner Jimmy Hurwitz] in late 1993. They needed a part-time guy for Sundays to help in the humidor and mix pipe tobacco. Sundays turned into a full-time job within six months, and I became their chief cigar buyer.'[7] His cigars were first made in Little Havana in Miami, but production has since expanded into Nicaragua. Even if you do not much care for body art, be prepared to suspend your prejudices, as Tattoo Pete has proved to be a far more talented cigar maker than he was bass guitarist and strip-club bouncer; his cigars are often highly rated in tastings.

STRENGTH: Champion arm wrestler

FLAVOUR: Earthy

CHARACTER: Surprisingly sophisticated

BEST ENJOYED: By those who like to mix tattoos and tobacco

---

[7]   David Savona, 'Straight Talking with Pete Johnson',
       Cigar Aficionado, May/June 2012

NOTABLE NEW WORLD BRANDS IN BRIEF

GURKHA

In 1887, so the story told by Gurkha goes, British soldiers in the colonies began to smoke cigars made with local tobacco, and somehow these cigars got to bear the name of the legendary Nepalese fighters. The modern story is even more intriguing. In 1988, Kaizad Hansotia, an Indian man raised in Hong Kong and London and active in the luxury watch business, was relaxing on the beach in Goa when he met a man selling cigars under the brand name Gurkha. Hansotia enjoyed the cigars and, in Victor Kiam style, ended up buying the entire stock and the cigar brand for $143.

Since their launch in 1989, they have come to personify cigar bling, with extravagant packaging and ambitious pricing: His Majesty's Reserve costs $25,000 for a box of 20; steep, even though although an entire bottle of Louis XIII cognac is said to have been used to 'infuse' these cigars. Equally imaginative are the names, with *vitolas* called among other things Hedonism and Kraken, while the lines of cigars

bear names such as Gurkha Warlord, Gurkha Assassin, Gurkha Evil, Gurkha Genghis Khan, Gurkha Special Ops (including waterproof case and commando knife; tagline, 'Only Made For the Brave') and the pleasingly alliterative Gurkha Ghost. But even the relatively simply named cigars such as the Gurkha Heritage are lively and polyglot in the tobaccos they use, with leaf from Ecuador, Nicaragua, the Dominican Republic and Pennsylvania.

LA AURORA

The Domincan Republic's longest-established cigar brand, La Aurora was founded on 3 October 1903 by 18-year-old Eduardo León Jimenes, son and grandson of tobacco growers. Over a century later, the company's various brands – La Aurora, León Jimenes, Princes, Family Reserve and Imperiales – are sold in over 70 countries, and the workforce, originally half a dozen, now tops 1,000.

LA FLOR DOMINICANA

As the name suggests, La Flor Dominicana is based in the Dominican Republic. Founded in 1996 in Santiago, it prides itself on its vertical integration: the majority of the tobacco used – filler, binder and wrapper – is grown on its own farms and made into cigars in its own factory.

⚜ MY FATHER ⚜

The García family, who make Tatuaje Cigars [*q.v.*, page 221] for Pete Johnson, also have their own brand. José Pepin García emigrated from Cuba to the US in 2003 and set up a small factory in Miami's Little Havana; since then he has captured the palates of American cigar lovers. My Father cigars were born out of a secret project that Pepin's son Jaime had blended in Nicaragua as a tribute to his father. This exercise in filial devotion has now become a much-respected boutique brand in the US.

⚜ OLIVA ⚜

The Oliva Cigar Company can trace its origins back to nine-teenth-century Cuba, where Melanio Oliva and his son Hipolito grew tobacco. Hipolito's son Gilberto entered tobacco broking, leaving Cuba in the 1960s first for Spain before even-tually settling in Nicaragua, where he grew tobacco and made cigars (working at one time for Nestor Plasencia).

In 1996, Gilberto and his son Gilberto Jr formed their own business, and after some lean years have emerged as one of the great Central American cigar dynasties, with such commercial successes as Nubs – the fat, stumpy little time-optimised cigars that are a maximum four inches in length but boast ring gauges from the mid-50s to the mid-60s. Apparently the idea was to dispense with the foreplay of flavour and aroma development that occurs during the cigar's first third, and instead join it at what many regard as the peak of its flavour. Another concept that has proved popular with the trend-hungry American market is the Cain, a powerhouse chainsaw of a cigar made of *ligero* leaf, the flagship cigar of which has been the Cain Daytona. Unsurprisingly, Nub and Cain have been combined in a sort of *Alien vs. Predator* ultimate powerhouse – the Cain Nub.

⟨ PLASENCIA ⟩

Nestor Plasencia Sr is a tobacco grower and cigar maker of Cuban descent, with farms and factories in Honduras and Nicaragua. His company produces over 35 million cigars a yearlxxiv (some estimates run as high as 38 million); in addition, his fields and factories supply a remarkable array of brands – La Invicta, Alec Bradley, Gurkha and Rocky Patel – making him one of the leading figures in Central American tobacco.

Plasencia farms over 3,000 acres of tobacco, half of which is worked on by small growers under contract to the company. The majority of the land is in Nicaragua, with some plantations in other countries around the region, including Panama and Costa Rica. Plasencia, also a pioneer in organically cultivated tobacco, enjoys a high reputation for quality.

⟨ ROCKY PATEL ⟩

One of the most colourful newcomers to the cigar market, during the mid-1990s Rocky Patel was a Los Angeles entertainment and product liability lawyer by profession, but a cigar impressario by vocation. In 1996, he launched the Indian Tabac Cigar Co. and caught customers' eyes and imaginations with his polychromatic packaging. Hummingbird-bright livery aside, Patel's cigars tend to be blended across countries; his belief is that this delivers a more complex and intriguing cigar.

He made his name in 2003 with the low-volume Rocky Patel Vintage series, made with aged tobaccos, including some 'forgotten' bales of old Honduran and Ecuadorean leaf. More recently he pulled off a great coup when he hired crack Cuban cigar roller Hamlet Paredes, whom I first met at the Romeo y Julieta factory in Havana at the beginning of the century. The majority of the 14 million or so cigars that Patel makes every year are produced in the factories of Nestor Plasencia.

APPENDIX A

LIMITED EDITIONS of HAVANA CIGARS

Cigar sizes are given as
RING GAUGE × LENGTH

2000/01

BRAND	VITOLA DE GALERA	PACK	SIZE
Partagás	Pirámides	25	52 × 6⅛ in/156 mm
Montecristo	Robusto	25	50 × 4⅛ in/105 mm
Romeo y Julieta	Prominente (DC)	25	49 × 7⅝ in/194 mm
Hoyo	Particulares	5	47 × 9¼ in/235 mm

2001/02

BRAND	VITOLA DE GALERA	PACK	SIZE
Cohiba	Pirámides	25	52 × 6⅛ in/156 mm
Romeo y Julieta	Robustos	25	50 × 4⅞ in/124 mm
Partagás	D3 (dressed box)	25	46 × 5½ in/140 mm
Hoyo	Particulares	5	47 × 9¼ in/234 mm
Montecristo	Double Corones	25	49 × 7⅝ in/194 mm

2003

BRAND	VITOLA DE GALERA	PACK	SIZE
Hoyo	Pirámides	25	52 × 6⅛ in/156 mm
Partagás	D2	25	48 × 6⅝ in/168 mm
Romeo y Julieta	Hermosos No.1	25	48 × 6⅝ in/168 mm
Montecristo	C	25	46 × 5⅝ in/143 mm
Cohiba	Double Coronas	25	49 × 7⅝ in/194 mm

2004

BRAND	VITOLA DE GALERA	PACK	SIZE
Partagás	D1	25	50 × 6¾ in/171 mm
Romeo y Julieta	Hermosos No.2	25	48 × 6¼ in/159 mm
Cohiba	Sublimes	25	54 × 6½ in/165 mm
Hoyo	Epicure Especial	25	50 × 5½ in/140 mm

2005

BRAND	VITOLA DE GALERA	PACK	SIZE
H. Upmann	Magnum 50	25	50 × 6½ in/165 mm
Romeo y Julieta	Petit Pirámides	25	50 × 5 in/127 mm
Montecristo	D (3-4-3)	10	43 × 6¾ in/171 mm

2006

BRAND	VITOLA DE GALERA	PACK	SIZE
Partagás	D3 (SBN)	25	46 × 5½ in/140 mm
Cohiba	Pirámides	10	52 × 6⅛ in/156 mm
Montecristo	Robusto (SBN)	25	50 × 4⅞ in/124 mm

2007

BRAND	VITOLA DE GALERA	PACK	SIZE
Hoyo	Regalos	25	46 × 5⅜ in/137 mm
Romeo y Julieta	Escudos	25	50 × 5½ in/140 mm
Trinidad	Ingenios	12	42 × 6½ in/165 mm

2008

BRAND	VITOLA DE GALERA	PACK	SIZE
Montecristo	Sublimes	10	54 × 6½ in/165 mm
Cuaba	Pirámides	10	52 × 6⅛ in/156 mm
Partagás	Series D No.5	25	50 × 4⅜ in/110 mm

2009

BRAND	VITOLA DE GALERA	PACK	SIZE
Romeo	Dukes	10	54 × 5½ in/140 mm
H. Upmann	Magnum 48	25	48 × 4⅜ in/110 mm
Bolívar	Petit Belicosos	25	52 × 5 in/127 mm

2010

BRAND	VITOLA DE GALERA	PACK	SIZE
Montecristo	Grand Edmundo	10	50 × 5⅞ in/140 mm
Partagás	Serie D Especial	10	50 × 5½ in/140 mm
Trinidad	Short Robusto T	12	50 × 4 in/102 mm

2011

BRAND	VITOLA DE GALERA	PACK	SIZE
Cohiba	1966	10	52 × 6½ in/165 mm
Hoyo	Short Pirámides	10	46 × 5⅜ in/137 mm
Ramón Allones	Allones Extra	25	44 × 5⅝ in/143 mm

2012

BRAND	VITOLA DE GALERA	PACK	SIZE
H. Upmann	Robusto	25	50 × 4⅞ in/124 mm
Partagás	Serie C No.3	10	48 × 5½ in/140 mm
Montecristo	520	10	55 × 6⅛ in/156 mm

2013

BRAND	VITOLA DE GALERA	PACK	SIZE
Punch	Serie d'Oro No. 2	25	52 × 5½ in/140 mm
Hoyo	Grand Epicure	10	55 × 5¼ in/133 mm
Romeo y Julieta	Romeo Deluxe	10	52 × 6⅜ in/162 mm

2014

BRAND	VITOLA DE GALERA	PACK	SIZE
Bolívar	Super Coronas	25	48 × 5½ in/140 mm
Partagás	Selección Privada	10	50 × 6¼ in/159 mm
Cohiba	Robusto Supremos	10	58 × 5 in/127 mm

2015

BRAND	VITOLA DE GALERA	PACK	SIZE
H. Upmann	Magnum 56	25	56 × 5⅞ in/149 mm
Ramón Allones	Club Allones	10	47 × 5⅜ in/137 mm

2016

BRAND	VITOLA DE GALERA	PACK	SIZE
Trinidad	Topes	12	56 × 5 in/127 mm
Montecristo	Dantes	10	48 × 6½ in/165 mm
Romeo y Julieta	Verona	25	53 × 6½ in/165 mm

APPENDIX B

REGIONAL EDITIONS of HAVANA CIGARS

Cigar sizes are given as

RING GAUGE × LENGTH

2004

BRAND	VITOLA DE SALIDA	VIT. GALERA	SIZE	COUNTRY
Ramón Allones	Bellicosos Finos 2004	Campanas	52 × 5½ in/140 mm	UK

2005

BRAND	VITOLA DE SALIDA	VIT. GALERA	SIZE	COUNTRY
Bolívar	Gold Medal	Cervantes	42 × 6½ in/165 mm	Germany
Punch	Robustos	Robustos	50 × 4⅞ in/124 mm	Switzerland
Punch	Superfinos	Minutos	42 × 4⅜ in/110 mm	Italy
Ramón Allones	Eminencia	Franciscos	44 × 5⅝ in/143 mm	Italy
Ramón Allones	Selección Suprema	Coronas Gordas	46 × 5⅝ in/143 mm	Switzerland

2006

BRAND	VITOLA DE SALIDA	VIT. GALERA	SIZE	COUNTRY
Bolívar	Colosales	Dobles	50 × 6⅛ in/155 mm	Germany
Bolívar	Libertador	Sublimes	54 × 6½ in/165 mm	France
Juan López	Obus	Campanas	52 × 5½ in/140 mm	France
Por Larrañaga	Lonsdale	Cervantes	42 × 6½ in/165 mm	Germany
Punch	Super Robustos del Punch	Dobles	50 × 6⅛ in/155 mm	Asia-Pacific
Ramón Allones	Estupendos	Julieta No.2	47 × 7 in/178 mm	Asia-Pacific

2007

BRAND	VITOLA DE SALIDA	VIT. GALERA	SIZE	COUNTRY
Bolívar	Double Coronas	Prominentes	49 × 7⅝ in/194 mm	Middle East
Bolívar	Simones	Hermosos No.4	48 × 5 in/127 mm	Canada
Edmundo Dantes	El Conde 109	109	50 × 7¼ in/184 mm	Mexico
El Rey del Mundo	Vikingos	Gordito	50 × 5½ in/140 mm	Baltic
Por Larrañaga	Magnifico	Partagás 16	50 × 6¾ in/170 mm	UK
Por Larrañaga	Robustos de Larrañaga	Robustos	50 × 4⅞ in/124 mm	Asia-Pacific
Ramón Allones	Gran Robusto	Dobles	47 × 6⅛ in/155 mm	Belgium & Luxemburg
Vegas Robaina	Maestros	Gordito	50 × 5½ in/140 mm	Spain

2008

BRAND	VITOLA DE SALIDA	VIT. GALERA	SIZE	COUNTRY
Bolívar	Armonia	Salomon	57 × 7¼ in/184 mm	China
Bolívar	Legendarios	Dobles	50 × 6⅛ in/155 mm	Switzerland
Bolívar	Petit Libertador	Petit Robustos	50 × 4 in/102 mm	France
Bolívar	Short Bolívar	Petit Edmundo	52 × 4⅜ in/110 mm	Asia-Pacific
El Rey del Mundo	Torpedo	Campanas	52 × 5½ in/140 mm	Italy
Juan López	Maximo	Hermosos No.2	48 × 6⅛ in/155 mm	Switzerland
Juan López	Short Torpedo	Petit Pirámides	50 × 5 in/127 mm	Caribbean Sea
La Gloria Cubana	Gloriosos	Dobles	50 × 6⅛ in/155 mm	UK
Por Larrañaga	Belicosos Extra	Campanas	52 × 5½ in/140 mm	France
Punch	Robustos	Robustos	50 × 4⅞ in/124 mm	Arab Emirates
Punch	Serie d'Oro No.1	Pirámides	52 × 6⅛ in/155 mm	UK
Ramón Allones	Especial de Allones	Campanas	52 × 5½ in/140 mm	France
Ramón Allones	Grandes	Paco	49 × 7⅛ in/180 mm	Spain
Ramón Allones	Phoenicios	Sublimes	54 × 6½ in/165 mm	Middle East
Vegas Robaina	Marshall	Robustos	50 × 4⅞ in/124 mm	Adriatic Sea
Vegas Robaina	Petit Robustos	Petit Robustos	50 × 4 in/102 mm	Portugal

2009

BRAND	VITOLA DE SALIDA	VIT. GALERA	SIZE	COUNTRY
Bolívar	5th. Avenida	109	50 × 7¼ in/184 mm	Germany
Bolívar	El Greco	Gordito	50 × 5½ in/140 mm	Greece & Cyprus
Bolívar	Especiales No.2	Delicados	38 × 7½ in/192 mm	Germany

2009

BRAND	VITOLA DE SALIDA	VIT. GALERA	SIZE	COUNTRY
Bolívar	Fabulosos	Edmundo	52 × 5¼ in/135 mm	Belgium & Luxemburg
El Rey del Mundo	Balthasar	Dobles	50 × 6⅛ in/155 mm	Baltic
El Rey del Mundo	Choix de l'Epoque	Petit Edmundo	52 × 4⅜ in/110 mm	UK
El Rey del Mundo	Petit Compañía	Petit Pirámides	50 × 5 in/127 mm	France
Juan López	Selección Suprema	Torre Iznaga	52 × 6⅝ in/170 mm	UK
Juan López	Short Robusto	Petit Robustos	50 × 4 in/102 mm	Andorra
Por Larrañaga	Los Andes	Petit Pirámides	50 × 5 in/127 mm	Peru, Chile & Bolivia
Por Larrañaga	Valiosos	Pirámides	52 × 6⅛ in/155 mm	Switzerland
Punch	Diamedas Extra	Diademas	55 × 9⅛ in/233 mm	Italy
Punch	Gran Robusto	Dobles	50 × 6⅛ in/155 mm	Spain
Punch	Northern Lights	Petit Edmundo	52 × 4⅜ in/110 mm	Nordic region
Punch	Platino	Prominentes	49 × 7⅝ in/194 mm	India
Punch	Poderosos	Sublimes	54 × 6½ in/164 mm	Switzerland
Punch	Punch Royal	Gordito	50 × 5½ in/140 mm	Belgium & Luxemburg
Punch	Small Club	Petit Robustos	50 × 4 in/102 mm	France
Ramón Allones	Beritus	Edmundo	52 × 5¼ in/135 mm	Libano
Ramón Allones	Celestiales Finos	Britanicas	46 × 5⅜ in/137 mm	Asia-Pacific
Ramón Allones	Petit Unicos	Petit Pirámides	50 × 5 in/127 mm	Canada
Saint Luis Rey	Pacificos	Pirámides	52 × 6⅛ in/155 mm	Asia-Pacific
Vegas Robaina	Petit Robaina	Petit Edmundo	52 × 4⅜ in/110 mm	Canada

2010

BRAND	VITOLA DE SALIDA	VIT. GALERA	SIZE	COUNTRY
Bolívar	108	Coronas Gordas	46 × 5⅝ in/143 mm	Spain
Bolívar	Bolívar B-2	Pirámides	52 × 6⅛ in/155 mm	Canada
Bolívar	Distinguidos	Romeo	52 × 6⅜ in/162 mm	China
Bolívar	Emiratos	Sublimes	54 × 6½ in/165 mm	Arab Emirates
El Rey del Mundo	Elegantes	Gordito	50 × 5½ in/140 mm	Switzerland
Fonseca	Fonseca No.4	Hermosos No.4	48 × 5 in/127 mm	Belgium & Luxemburg
Juan López	Selección No.5	Perlas	50 × 4 in/102 mm	Andorra
Juan López	Selección No.3	Petit Edmundo	52 × 4⅜ in/110 mm	Belgium & Luxemburg
Juan López	Selección No.4	Pirámides	52 × 6⅛ in/155 mm	Asia-Pacific

2010

BRAND	VITOLA DE SALIDA	VIT. GALERA	SIZE	COUNTRY
La Flor de Cano	Short Robusto	Petit Robustos	50 × 4 in/102 mm	UK
La Gloria Cubana	Triunfos	Magnum 50	50 × 6¼ in/160 mm	Switzerland
Por Larrañaga	Encantos	Dalias	43 × 6⅝ in/170 mm	Asia-Pacific
Por Larrañaga	Regalias de Londres	Gordito	50 × 5½ in/140 mm	UK
Por Larrañaga	Robustos	Robustos	50 × 4⅞ in/124 mm	Germany
Punch	Petit Pirámides	Petit Pirámides	50 × 5 in/127 mm	South Africa
Ramón Allones	Belicosos	Campanas	52 × 5½ in/140 mm	Germany
Ramón Allones	Gladiator	Torre Iznaga	52 × 6⅝ in/170 mm	Peru, Chile & Bolivia
Ramón Allones	Gordito de Allones	Gordito	50 × 5½ in/140 mm	Canada
Ramón Allones	Lusitanos	Petit Edmundo	52 × 4⅜ in/110 mm	Portugal
Ramón Allones	Phoenicios 32	Pirámides	52 × 6⅛ in/155 mm	Libano
Sancho Panza	Quijote	Prominentes	49 × 7⅝ in/194 mm	Spain
Vegas Robaina	Petit Robustos	Petit Robustos	50 × 4 in/102 mm	France

2011

BRAND	VITOLA DE SALIDA	VIT. GALERA	SIZE	COUNTRY
Bolívar	681	Sobresalientes	53 × 6¼ in/153 mm	Bulgaria
Bolívar	Britanicas	Britanicas Extra	48 × 5⅜ in/137 mm	UK
Bolívar	Emperador	Hermosos No.2	48 × 6⅛ in/157 mm	Russia
Bolívar	Oryx	Edmundo	52 × 5¼ in/135 mm	Qatar
Edmundo Dantes	Conde 54	Sublimes	54 × 6½ in/165 mm	Mexico
El Rey del Mundo	NL No.1	Mágicos	52 × 4½ in/115 mm	Netherlands
Fonseca	Amateur	Gordito	50 × 5½ in/140 mm	France
Juan López	Distinguidos	Romeo	52 × 6⅜ in/162 mm	Germany
Juan López	Ideales	Petit Robustos	50 × 4 in/102 mm	Austria
Juan López	Supreme	Edmundo	52 × 5¼ in/135 mm	Canada
La Escepcion	Selectos Finos	Parejos	38 × 6½ in/165 mm	Italy
La Glora Cubana	Belux No.1	Genios	52 × 5½ in/140 mm	Belgium & Luxemburg
Por Larrañaga	Legendarios	Partagás 16	50 × 6⅝ in/170 mm	Spain
Punch	Descobridores	Robustos	50 × 4⅞ in/124 mm	Portugal
Punch	Sabrosos	Pirámides	52 × 6⅛ in/155 mm	Asia-Pacific
Punch	Clasicos	109	50 × 7½ in/184 mm	Switzerland
Quai d'Orsay	Superiores	Robustos	50 × 4⅞ in/124 mm	Asia-Pacific
Quai d'Orsay	Robusto Embajador	Mágicos	52 × 4½ in/115 mm	France
Ramón Allones	Especiales	Mágicos	52 × 4½ in/115 mm	Switzerland

2011

BRAND	VITOLA DE SALIDA	VIT. GALERA	SIZE	COUNTRY
Ramón Allones	Macedonian	Edmundo	52 × 5¼ in/135 mm	Greece & Cyprus
Ramón Allones	Petit Robusto	Petit Robustos	50 × 4 in/102 mm	Israel
Ramón Allones	Super Ramon	Rodolfo	54 × 7⅛ in/180 mm	Canada
Sancho Panza	Escuderos	Dobles	50 × 6⅛ in/155 mm	Germany

2012

BRAND	VITOLA DE SALIDA	VIT. GALERA	SIZE	COUNTRY
Diplomaticos	Colección Privada I	Petit Robustos	50 × 4 in/102 mm	Spain
Rey del Mundo	Aniversario	Geniales	54 × 5⅞ in/150 mm	Asia-Pacific
Por Larrañaga	Small Robustos	Petit Robustos	50 × 4 in/102 mm	Italy
Punch	Sir John	Hermosos No.4	48 × 5 in/127 mm	Germany
Ramón Allones	Petit Belicosos	Petit Belicosos	52 × 4⅞ in/124 mm	UK
Ramón Allones	Eshmoun	Sunlimes	54 × 6½ in/165 mm	Libano
Vegas Robaina	Petit Unicos	Petit Belicosos	52 × 4⅞ in/124 mm	Switzerland
Vegas Robaina	XV Anniversario	Sublimes	54 × 6½ in/165 mm	Canada

2013

BRAND	VITOLA DE SALIDA	VIT. GALERA	SIZE	COUNTRY
Bolívar	Poderosos	Rodolfo	54 × 7⅛ in/180 mm	Belgium & Luxemburg
Bolívar	Presidente	Geniales	54 × 5⅞ in/150 mm	Switzerland
Bolívar	Redentor	Mágicos	52 × 4½ in/115 mm	Brasil
El Rey del Mundo	Infantes	Robusto	50 × 4⅞ in/124 mm	Cuba
Juan López	Minutos	Minutos	42 × 4⅜ in/110 mm	France
La Flor de Cano	Grandiosos	Edmundo	52 × 4⅞ in/124 mm	Asia-Pacific
La Flor de Cano	Gran Cano	Gordito	50 × 6½ in/140 mm	UK
Por Larrañaga	Secretos	Secretos	40 × 4⅜ in/110 mm	Spain
Quai d'Orsay	Belicoso Royal	Petit Belicosos	52 × 5 in/127 mm	France
Rafael Gonzalez	Petit Pirámides	Petit Pirámides	50 × 5 in/127 mm	Germany
Ramón Allones	Sidon	Sobresalientes	53 × 6 in/152 mm	Libano
Ramón Allones	Petit Allones	Petit Edmundo	52 × 4⅜ in/110 mm	Andorra
Ramón Allones	Robusto Corto	Petit Robustos	50 × 4 in/102 mm	Netherlands

2014

BRAND	VITOLA DE SALIDA	VIT. GALERA	SIZE	COUNTRY
Bolívar	Bosphorus	Petit Edmundo	52 × 4⅜ in/110 mm	Turkey
Diplomaticos	Bushida	109	54 × 5⅞ in/150 mm	Asia-Pacific
Juan López	Chiado 1864	Petit Robustos	52 × 4½ in/115 mm	Portugal
Juan López	Don Juan	Edmundo	52 × 5¼ in/135 mm	Belgium & Luxemburg

2014

BRAND	VITOLA DE SALIDA	VIT. GALERA	SIZE	COUNTRY
La Flor de Cano	Siboney	Minutos	42 × 4⅜ in/110 mm	Canada
La Gloria Cubana	Paraiso	Edmundo	52 × 5¼ in/135 mm	Caribbean Sea
Por Larrañaga	Sobresalientes	Sobresalientes	53 × 6 in/152 mm	UK
Ramón Allones	898	Dalias	43 × 6⅝ in/170 mm	Germany
Ramón Allones	Short Perfectos	Petit Pirámides	50 × 5 in/127 mm	Italy
Ramón Allones	Sur	Genios	52 × 5½ in/140 mm	Libano
Ramón Allones	Perfectos	Britanicas Extra	48 × 5⅜ in/137 mm	Switzerland
Ramón Allones	Caprichos	Mágicos	52 × 4½ in/115 mm	Spain
Saint Luis Rey	Inca	Petit Robustos	50 × 4 in/102 mm	Peru, Chile & Bolivia
Sancho Panza	Eslavo	109	50 × 7¼ in/184 mm	Serbia
Vegas Robaina	Short Robaina	Minutos	42 × 4⅜ in/110 mm	Andorra

2015

BRAND	VITOLA DE SALIDA	VIT. GALERA	SIZE	COUNTRY
Bolívar	Belgravia	Montesco	54 × 5⅛ in/130 mm	UK
Bolívar	Emarati	Edmundo	52 × 5¼ in/135 mm	Arab Emirates
Diplomaticos	El Embajador	Edmundo	52 × 5¼ in/135 mm	Canada
Diplomaticos	Excelencia	Robustos	50 × 4⅞ in/124 mm	Cuba
El Rey del Mundo	Petit Robustos	Petit Robustos	50 × 4 in/102 mm	Spain
Juan López	Malecon	Montesco	55 × 5⅛ in/130 mm	Andorra
La Escepción	Don José	Hermosos No.4	48 × 5 in/127 mm	Italy
La Gloria Cubana	Glorias	Rodolfo	54 × 7⅛ in/180 mm	Germany
La Gloria Cubana	Revolution	Montesco	55 × 5⅛ in/130 mm	Asia-Pacific
Por Larrañaga	Opera	Mágicos	48 × 5 in/127 mm	Cuba
Punch	Supremos	Sobresalientes	53 × 6 in/152 mm	Switzerland
Quai d'Orsay	Robusto Diplomatico	Hermosos No.4	48 × 5 in/127 mm	France
Ramón Allones	Phoenicios	Montesco	55 × 5⅛ in/130 mm	Libano
Ramón Allones	Anniversario 225	Gorditos	50 × 5⅝ in/141 mm	UK

BRAND	VITOLA DE SALIDA	VIT. GALERA	SIZE	COUNTRY
Bolívar	Tesoro	Salomon	57 × 7¼ in/184 mm	Germany
Bolívar	Byblos	Mágicos	52 × 4½ in/115 mm	Libano
Edmundo Dantes	Conde Belicoso	Campanas	52 × 5½ in/140 mm	Mexico
El Rey del Mundo	Choix du Roi	Montesco	55 × 5⅛ in/130 mm	Belgium & Luxemburg
Juan López	Eminentes	Sublimes	54 × 6½ in/165 mm	Switzerland
Juan López	Selección Superba	Magnum 50	50 × 6¼ in/160 mm	UK
La Flor de Cano	Casanova	Demitasse	32 × 3⅞ in/100 mm	Italy
La Gloria Cubana	Platinum Edition	Duke	54 × 5½ in/140 mm	Netherlands
Quai d'Orsay	Secreto Cubano	Secretos	40 × 4⅜ in/110 mm	France
Rafael Gonzalez	88	Britanicas Extra	48 × 5⅜ in/137 mm	Asia-Pacific
Ramón Allones	Hexagone	Duke	54 × 5½ in/140 mm	France
Ramón Allones	Terra Magica	Dobles	50 × 6⅛ in/155 mm	Croatia & Slovenia
Ramón Allones	La Palmera	Sublimes	54 × 6½ in/165 mm	Arab Emirates
Ramón Allones	Patagon	Petit Edmundo	52 × 4⅜ in/110 mm	Argentina
Saint Luis Rey	Tesoros	Petit Edmundo	52 × 4⅜ in/110 mm	Spain
Sain Luis Rey	Marquez	Geniales	54 × 5⅞ in/150 mm	Cuba

APPENDIX C

WIDELY AVAILABLE STANDARD SIZES of HAVANA CIGARS

Cigar sizes are given as
RING GAUGE × LENGTH

Formats: DF = Double Figurado   F = Figurado   P = Parejo   Pt = Pigtail

BRAND
⟨ *BOLÍVAR* ⟩

VITOLA DE SALIDA	VITOLA DE GALERA	FORMAT	SIZE
Belicosos Finos	Campanas	F	52 × 5½ in/140 mm
Belicosos Finos	Campanas	F	52 × 5½ in/140 mm
Bolívar Tubos No.1	Coronas	P	42 × 5⅜ in/142 mm
Bolívar Tubos No.2	Marevas	P	42 × 5⅛ in/129 mm
Bolívar Tubos No.3	Placeras	P	34 × 4⅞ in/125 mm
Coronas Gigantes	Julieta No.2	P	47 × 7 in/178 mm
Coronas Junior	Minutos	P	42 × 4⅜ in/110 mm
Petit Coronas	Marevas	P	42 × 5⅛ in/129 mm
Royal Coronas	Robustos	P	50 × 4⅞ in/124 mm
Royal Coronas	Robustos	P	50 × 4⅞ in/124 mm

BRAND
⟨ *COHIBA* ⟩

VITOLA DE SALIDA	VITOLA DE GALERA	FORMAT	SIZE
BHK 56	Laguito No.6	Pt	56 × 6½ in/166 mm
BHK 54	Laguito No.5	Pt	54 × 5¾ in/144 mm
BHK 52	Laguito No.4	Pt	52 × 4⅝ in/119 mm
Coronas Especiales	Laguito No.2	Pt	38 × 6 in/152 mm
Coronas Especiales	Laguito No.2	Pt	38 × 6 in/152 mm
Esplendidos	Julieta No.2	P	47 × 7 in/178 mm

⟨ *COHIBA* ⟩

VITOLA DE SALIDA	VITOLA DE GALERA	FORMAT	SIZE
Esplendidos	Julieta No.2	P	47 × 7 in/178 mm
Exquisitos	Seoane	P	33 × 5 in/126 mm
Exquisitos	Seoane	P	33 × 5 in/126 mm
Genios	Genios 5	P	52 × 5½ in/140 mm
Genios	Genios 5	P	52 × 5½ in/140 mm
Lanceros	Laguito No.1	Pt	38 × 7½ in/192 mm
Mágicos	Mágicos 5	P	52 × 4½ in/115 mm
Mágicos	Mágicos 5	P	52 × 4½ in/115 mm
Medio Siglo	Medio Siglo	P	52 × 4 in/102 mm
Medio Siglo	Medio Siglo	P	52 × 4 in/102 mm
Panetelas	Laguito No.3	P	26 × 4½ in/115 mm
Panetelas	Laguito No.3	P	26 × 4½ in/115 mm
Pirámides Extra	Pirámides Extra	F	54 × 6¼ in/160 mm
Pirámides Extra	Pirámides Extra	F	54 × 6¼ in/160 mm
Robustos	Robustos	P	50 × 4⅞ in/124 mm
Robustos	Robustos	P	50 × 4⅞ in/124 mm
Robustos	Robustos	P	50 × 4⅞ in/124 mm
Secretos	Secretos 5	P	40 × 4⅜ in/110 mm
Secretos	Secretos 5	P	40 × 4⅜ in/110 mm
Siglo I	Perlas	P	40 × 4 in/102 mm
Siglo I	Perlas	P	40 × 4 in/102 mm
Siglo I	Perlas	P	40 × 4 in/102 mm
Siglo II	Marevas	P	42 × 5⅛ in/129 mm
Siglo II	Marevas	P	42 × 5⅛ in/129 mm
Siglo II	Marevas	P	42 × 5⅛ in/129 mm
Siglo III	Coronas Grandes	P	42 × 6⅛ in/155 mm
Siglo III	Coronas Grandes	P	42 × 6⅛ in/155 mm
Siglo III	Coronas Grandes	P	42 × 6⅛ in/155 mm
Siglo IV	Coronas Gordas	P	46 × 5⅝ in/143 mm
Siglo IV	Coronas Gordas	P	46 × 5⅝ in/143 mm
Siglo IV	Coronas Gordas	P	46 × 5⅝ in/143 mm
Siglo V	Dalias	P	43 × 6¾ in/170 mm
Siglo V	Dalias	P	43 × 6¾ in/170 mm
Siglo V	Dalias	P	43 × 6¾ in/170 mm
Siglo VI	Cañonazo	P	52 × 5⅞ in/150 mm
Siglo VI	Cañonazo	P	52 × 5⅞ in/150 mm
Siglo VI	Cañonazo	P	52 × 5⅞ in/150 mm

BRAND

COMBINACIONES

VITOLA DE SALIDA	VITOLA DE GALERA	FORMAT	SIZE
Selección Pirámides	Pirámides	F	52 × 6⅛ in/156 mm
Selección Robustos	Robustos	P	50 × 4⅞ in/124 mm
Selección Robustos	Robustos	P	50 × 4⅞ in/124 mm
Selección Pirámides	Pirámides	F	52 × 6⅛ in/156 mm
Selección Petit Robustos	Petit Robustos	P	50 × 4 in/102 mm

BRAND

CUABA

VITOLA DE SALIDA	VITOLA DE GALERA	FORMAT	SIZE
Distinguidos	Romeo	Df	52 × 6⅜ in/162 mm
Divinos	Petit Bouquet	Df	43 × 4 in/101 mm
Exclusivos	Exquisitos	Df	46 × 5¾ in 145 mm
Salomon	Salomon	Df	57 × 7¼ in/184 mm
Tradicionales	Favoritos	Df	42 × 4¾ in/120 mm

BRAND

DIPLOMATICOS

VITOLA DE SALIDA	VITOLA DE GALERA	FORMAT	SIZE
Diplomaticos No.2	Pirámides	F	52 × 6⅛ in/156 mm

BRAND

EL REY del MUNDO

VITOLA DE SALIDA	VITOLA DE GALERA	FORMAT	SIZE
Choix Supreme	Hermosos No.4	P	48 × 5 in/127 mm
Demi Tasse	Entreactos	P	30 × 3⅞ in/100 mm

BRAND

FONSECA

VITOLA DE SALIDA	VITOLA DE GALERA	FORMAT	SIZE
Cosaco	Cosacos	P	42 × 5⅜ in/135 mm
Delicias	Standard	P	40 × 4⅞ in/123 mm
Fonseca No.1	Cazadores	P	43 × 6⅜ in/162 mm
KDT Cadetes	Cadetes	P	36 × 4½ in/115 mm

◁ H. UPMANN ▷

VITOLA DE SALIDA	VITOLA DE GALERA	FORMAT	SIZE
Connoisseur No.1	Hermosos No.4	P	48×5 in/127 mm
Coronas Junior	Cadetes	P	$36 \times 4\frac{1}{2}$ in/115 mm
Coronas Major	Eminentes	P	$42 \times 5\frac{1}{4}$ in/132 mm
Coronas Minor	Coronitas	P	$40 \times 4\frac{5}{8}$ in/117 mm
Epicures	Epicures	P	$35 \times 4\frac{3}{8}$ in/110 mm
Magnum 46	Coronas Gordas	P	$46 \times 5\frac{5}{8}$ in/143 mm
Magnum 46	Coronas Gordas	P	$46 \times 5\frac{5}{8}$ in/143 mm
Magnum 50	Magnum 50	P	$50 \times 6\frac{1}{4}$ in/160 mm
Magnum 50	Magnum 50	P	$50 \times 6\frac{1}{4}$ in/160 mm
Magnum 50	Magnum 50	P	$50 \times 6\frac{1}{4}$ in/160 mm
Magnum 54	Magnum 54	P	$54 \times 4\frac{3}{4}$ in/120 mm
Magnum 54	Magnum 54	P	$54 \times 4\frac{3}{4}$ in/120 mm
Magnum 54	Magnum 54	P	$54 \times 4\frac{3}{4}$ in/120 mm
Majestic	Cremas	P	$40 \times 5\frac{1}{2}$ in/140 mm
Petit Coronas	Marevas	P	$42 \times 5\frac{1}{8}$ in/129 mm
Regalias	Petit Coronas	P	$42 \times 5\frac{1}{8}$ in/129 mm
Sir Winston	Julieta No.2	P	47×7 in/178 mm
Upmann No.2	Pirámides	F	$52 \times 6\frac{1}{8}$ in/156 mm
Half Corona	Half Corona	P	$44 \times 3\frac{1}{2}$ in/90 mm
Half Corona	Half Corona	P	$44 \times 3\frac{1}{2}$ in/90 mm

◁ HOYO de MONTERREY ▷

VITOLA DE SALIDA	VITOLA DE GALERA	FORMAT	SIZE
Coronations	Petit Coronas	P	$42 \times 5\frac{1}{8}$ in/129 mm
Coronations	Petit Coronas	P	$42 \times 5\frac{1}{8}$ in/129 mm
Double Coronas	Prominentes	P	$49 \times 7\frac{5}{8}$ in/194 mm
Double Coronas	Prominentes	P	$49 \times 7\frac{5}{8}$ in/194 mm
Epicure Especial	Gordito	P	$50 \times 5\frac{1}{2}$ in/141 mm
Epicure Especial	Gordito	P	$50 \times 5\frac{1}{2}$ in/141 mm
Epicure Especial	Gordito	P	$50 \times 5\frac{1}{2}$ in/141 mm
Epicure No.1	Coronas Gordas	P	$46 \times 5\frac{5}{8}$ in 143 mm
Epicure No.1	Coronas Gordas	P	$46 \times 5\frac{5}{8}$ in 143 mm
Epicure No.2	Robustos	P	$50 \times 4\frac{7}{8}$ in/124 mm
Epicure No.2	Robustos	P	$50 \times 4\frac{7}{8}$ in/124 mm
Epicure No.2	Robustos	P	$50 \times 4\frac{7}{8}$ in/124 mm
Epicure No.2	Robustos	P	$50 \times 4\frac{7}{8}$ in/124 mm
Le Hoyo de San Juan	Geniales	P	$54 \times 5\frac{7}{8}$ in/150 mm
Le Hoyo de San Juan	Geniales	P	$54 \times 5\frac{7}{8}$ in/150 mm
Le Hoyo de San Juan	Geniales	P	$54 \times 5\frac{7}{8}$ in/150 mm

⊰ HOYO de MONTERREY ⊱

VITOLA DE SALIDA	VITOLA DE GALERA	FORMAT	SIZE
Le Hoyo du Député	Trabucos	P	$38 \times 4^{3}/_{8}$ in/110 mm
Le Hoyo du Maire	Entreactos	P	$30 \times 3^{7}/_{8}$ in/100 mm
Le Hoyo du Prince	Almuerzos	P	$40 \times 5^{1}/_{8}$ in/130 mm
Palmas Extra	Cremas	P	$40 \times 5^{1}/_{2}$ in/140 mm
Petit Robustos	Petit Robustos	P	50×4 in/102 mm
Petit Robustos	Petit Robustos	P	50×4 in/102 mm

⊰ JOSÉ L. PIEDRA ⊱

VITOLA DE SALIDA	VITOLA DE GALERA	FORMAT	SIZE
Brevas	Brevas JLP	P	$42 \times 5^{1}/_{4}$ in/133 mm
Brevas	Brevas JLP	P	$42 \times 5^{1}/_{4}$ in/133 mm
Cazadores	Cazadores JLP	P	43×6 in/152 mm
Cazadores	Cazadores JLP	P	43×6 in/152 mm
Conservas	Conservas JLP	P	$44 \times 5^{1}/_{2}$ in/140 mm
Conservas	Conservas JLP	P	$44 \times 5^{1}/_{2}$ in/140 mm
Cremas	Cremas JLP	P	$40 \times 5^{3}/_{8}$ in/136 mm
Cremas	Cremas JLP	P	$40 \times 5^{3}/_{8}$ in/136 mm
Petit Cazadores	Petit Cazadores	P	$43 \times 4^{1}/_{8}$ in/105 mm
Petit Cazadores	Petit Cazadores	P	$43 \times 4^{1}/_{8}$ in/105 mm
Petit Cetros	Petit Cetros JLP	P	38×5 in/127 mm
Petit Cetros	Petit Cetros JLP	P	38×5 in/127 mm

⊰ JUAN LÓPEZ ⊱

VITOLA DE SALIDA	VITOLA DE GALERA	FORMAT	SIZE
Selección No.1	Coronas Gordas	P	$46 \times 5^{5}/_{8}$ in/143 mm
Selección No.2	Robustos	P	$50 \times 4^{7}/_{8}$ in/124 mm

⊰ LA FLOR de CANO ⊱

VITOLA DE SALIDA	VITOLA DE GALERA	FORMAT	SIZE
Petit Coronas	Standard	P	$40 \times 4^{7}/_{8}$ in/123 mm
Selectos	Cristales	P	$41 \times 5^{7}/_{8}$ in/150 mm

⊰ LA GLORIA CUBANA ⊱

VITOLA DE SALIDA	VITOLA DE GALERA	FORMAT	SIZE
Medaille D'or No.4	Palmitas	P	32×6 in/152 mm

⊰ *MONTECRISTO* ⊱

VITOLA DE SALIDA	VITOLA DE GALERA	FORMAT	SIZE
Double Edmundo	Dobles	P	50 × 6$\frac{1}{8}$ in/155 mm
Double Edmundo	Dobles	P	50 × 6$\frac{1}{8}$ in/155 mm
Double Edmundo	Dobles	P	50 × 6$\frac{1}{8}$ in/155 mm
Eagle	Geniales	P	54 × 5$\frac{7}{8}$ in/150 mm
Eagle	Geniales	P	54 × 5$\frac{7}{8}$ in/150 mm
Edmundo	Edmundo	P	52 × 5$\frac{3}{8}$ in/135 mm
Edmundo	Edmundo	P	52 × 5$\frac{3}{8}$ in/135 mm
Edmundo	Edmundo	P	52 × 5$\frac{3}{8}$ in/135 mm
Joyitas	Laguito No.3	P	26 × 4$\frac{1}{2}$ in/115 mm
Junior	Trabucos	P	38 × 4$\frac{3}{8}$ in/110 mm
Junior	Trabucos	P	38 × 4$\frac{3}{8}$ in/110 mm
Master	Robustos	P	50 × 4$\frac{7}{8}$ in/124 mm
Master	Robustos	P	50 × 4$\frac{7}{8}$ in/124 mm
Media Corona	Half Corona	P	44 × 3$\frac{1}{2}$ in/90 mm
Media Corona	Half Corona	P	44 × 3$\frac{1}{2}$ in/90 mm
Montecristo A	Gran Corona	P	47 × 9$\frac{1}{4}$ in/235 mm
Especial	Laguito No.1	Pt	38 × 7$\frac{1}{2}$ in/192 mm
Especial No.2	Laguito No.2	Pt	38 × 6 in/152 mm
No.1	Cervantes	P	42 × 6$\frac{1}{2}$ in/165 mm
No.1	Cervantes	P	42 × 6$\frac{1}{2}$ in/165 mm
No.2	Pirámides	F	52 × 6$\frac{1}{8}$ in/156 mm
No.2	Pirámides	F	52 × 6$\frac{1}{8}$ in/156 mm
No.2	Pirámides	F	52 × 6$\frac{1}{8}$ in/156 mm
No.3	Coronas	P	42 × 5$\frac{5}{8}$ in/142 mm
No.3	Coronas	P	42 × 5$\frac{5}{8}$ in/142 mm
No.3	Coronas	P	42 × 5$\frac{5}{8}$ in/142 mm
No.4	Marevas	P	42 × 5$\frac{1}{8}$ in/129 mm
No.4	Marevas	P	42 × 5$\frac{1}{8}$ in/129 mm
No.4	Marevas	P	42 × 5$\frac{1}{8}$ in/129 mm
No.4	Marevas	P	42 × 5$\frac{1}{8}$ in/129 mm
No.5	Perlas	P	40 × 4 in/102 mm
No.5	Perlas	P	40 × 4 in/102 mm
No.5	Perlas	P	40 × 4 in/102 mm
Petit No.2	Petit No.2	F	52 × 4$\frac{3}{4}$ in/120 mm
Petit No.2	Petit No.2	F	52 × 4$\frac{3}{4}$ in/120 mm
Petit No.2	Petit No.2	F	52 × 4$\frac{3}{4}$ in/120 mm
Petit No.2	Petit No.2	F	52 × 4$\frac{3}{4}$ in/120 mm

⌦ *MONTECRISTO* ⌧

VITOLA DE SALIDA	VITOLA DE GALERA	FORMAT	SIZE
Petit No.2	Petit No.2	F	52 × 4³⁄₄ in/120 mm
Tubos	Coronas Grandes	P	42 × 6¹⁄₈ in/155 mm
Tubos	Coronas Grande	P	42 × 6¹⁄₈ in/155 mm
Petit Edmundo	Petit Edmundo	P	52 × 4³⁄₈ in/110 mm
Petit Edmundo	Petit Edmundo	P	52 × 4³⁄₈ in/110 mm
Petit Edmundo	Petit Edmundo	P	52 × 4³⁄₈ in/110 mm
Petit Tubos	Marevas	P	42 × 5¹⁄₈ in/129 mm
Petit Tubos	Marevas	P	42 × 5¹⁄₈ in/129 mm
Petit Tubos	Marevas	P	42 × 5¹⁄₈ in/129 mm
Petit Tubos	Marevas	P	42 × 5¹⁄₈ in/129 mm
Regata	Forum	F	46 × 5³⁄₈ in/135 mm
Regata	Forum	F	46 × 5³⁄₈ in/135 mm
80 Aniversario 2015	80 Aniversario	P	55 × 6¹⁄₂ in/165 mm

⌦ *PARTAGÁS* ⌧

VITOLA DE SALIDA	VITOLA DE GALERA	FORMAT	SIZE
8-9-8	Dalias	P	43 × 6³⁄₄ in/170 mm
Aristocrats	Petit Cetros	P	40 × 5¹⁄₈ in/129 mm
Capitols	Marevas	P	42 × 5¹⁄₈ in/129 mm
Coronas Junior	Coronitas	P	40 × 4⁵⁄₈ in/117 mm
Coronas Senior	Eminentes	P	42 × 5¹⁄₄ in/132 mm
Coronas Senior	Eminentes	P	42 × 5¹⁄₄ in/132 mm
Habaneros	Belvederes	P	39 × 4⁷⁄₈ in/125 mm
Lusitanias	Prominentes	P	49 × 7⁵⁄₈ in/194 mm
Lusitanias	Prominentes	P	49 × 7⁵⁄₈ in/194 mm
Lusitanias	Prominentes	P	49 × 7⁵⁄₈ in/194 mm
Mille Fleurs	Petit Coronas	P	42 × 5¹⁄₈ in/129 mm
Mille Fleurs	Petit Coronas	P	42 × 5¹⁄₈ in/129 mm
Mille Fleurs	Petit Coronas	P	42 × 5¹⁄₈ in/129 mm
Partagás De Luxe	Cremas	P	40 × 5¹⁄₂ in/140 mm
Partagás De Luxe	Cremas	P	40 × 5¹⁄₂ in/140 mm
Petit Coronas Especiales	Eminentes	P	42 × 5¹⁄₄ in/132 mm
Presidentes	Tacos	Df	47 × 6¹⁄₄ in/158 mm
Serie D No.4	Robustos	P	50 × 4⁷⁄₈ in/124 mm
Serie D No.4	Robustos	P	50 × 4⁷⁄₈ in/124 mm
Serie D No.4	Robustos	P	50 × 4⁷⁄₈ in/124 mm
Serie D No.6	D No.6	P	50 × 3¹⁄₂ in/90 mm
Serie D No.6	D No.6	P	50 × 3¹⁄₂ in/90 mm

❖ PARTAGÁS ❖

VITOLA DE SALIDA	VITOLA DE GALERA	FORMAT	SIZE
Serie P No.2	Pirámides	F	$52 \times 6\frac{1}{8}$ in/156 mm
Serie P No.2	Pirámides	F	$52 \times 6\frac{1}{8}$ in/156 mm
Serie P No.2	Pirámides	F	$52 \times 6\frac{1}{8}$ in/156 mm
Serie D No.5	D No.5	P	$50 \times 4\frac{3}{8}$ in/110 mm
Serie D No.5	D No.5	P	$50 \times 4\frac{3}{8}$ in/110 mm
Serie D No.5	D No.5	P	$50 \times 4\frac{3}{8}$ in/110 mm
Serie E No.2	Duke	P	$54 \times 5\frac{1}{2}$ in/140 mm
Serie E No.2	Duke	P	$54 \times 5\frac{1}{2}$ in/140 mm
Serie E No.2	Duke	P	$54 \times 5\frac{1}{2}$ in/140 mm
Shorts	Minutos	P	$42 \times 4\frac{3}{8}$ in/110 mm
Shorts	Minutos	P	$42 \times 4\frac{3}{8}$ in/110 mm
Super Partagás	Cremas	P	$40 \times 5\frac{1}{2}$ in/140 mm

❖ POR LARRAÑAGA ❖

VITOLA DE SALIDA	VITOLA DE GALERA	FORMAT	SIZE
8-9-8	Dalias	P	$43 \times 6\frac{3}{4}$ in/170 mm
Panetelas	Vegueritos	P	37×5 in/127 mm
Petit Coronas	Marevas	P	$42 \times 5\frac{1}{8}$ in/129 mm

❖ PUNCH ❖

VITOLA DE SALIDA	VITOLA DE GALERA	FORMAT	LONG
Coronations	Petit Coronas	P	$42 \times 5\frac{1}{8}$ in/129 mm
Double Coronas	Prominentes	P	$49 \times 7\frac{5}{8}$ in/194 mm
Double Coronas	Prominentes	P	$49 \times 7\frac{5}{8}$ in/194 mm
Petit Coronations	Coronitas	P	$40 \times 4\frac{5}{8}$ in/117 mm
Punch Punch	Coronas Gordas	P	$46 \times 5\frac{5}{8}$ in/143 mm
Punch Punch	Coronas Gordas	P	$46 \times 5\frac{5}{8}$ in/143 mm
Punch Punch	Coronas Gordas	P	$46 \times 5\frac{5}{8}$ in/143 mm
Royal Coronations	Conservas	P	$43 \times 5\frac{3}{4}$ in 145 mm

❖ QUAI d'ORSAY ❖

VITOLA DE SALIDA	VITOLA DE GALERA	FORMAT	SIZE
Coronas Claro	Coronas	P	$42 \times 5\frac{5}{8}$ in/142 mm

⊰ QUINTERO ⊱

VITOLA DE SALIDA	VITOLA DE GALERA	FORMAT	SIZE
Brevas	Nacionales	P	40 × 5½ in/140 mm
Favoritos	Conchas No.2	P	50 × 4½ in/115 mm
Favoritos	Conchas No.2	P	50 × 4½ in/115 mm
Londres Extra	Standard	P	40 × 4⅞ in/123 mm
Nacionales	Nacionales	P	40 × 5½ in/140 mm
Panetelas	Vegueritos	P	37 × 5 in/127 mm
Petit Quintero	Petit Cazadores	P	43 × 4 in/102 mm
Tubulares	Brevas JLP	P	42 × 5¼ in/133 mm

⊰ RAFAEL GONZALEZ ⊱

VITOLA DE SALIDA	VITOLA DE GALERA	FORMAT	SIZE
Panetelas Extra	Vegueritos	P	37 × 5 in/127 mm
Perlas	Perlas	P	40 × 4 in/102 mm
Perlas	Perlas	P	40 × 4 in/102 mm
Petit Coronas	Marevas	P	42 × 5⅛ in/129 mm

⊰ RAMÓN ALLONES ⊱

VITOLA DE SALIDA	VITOLA DE GALERA	FORMAT	SIZE
Specially Selected	Robustos	P	50 × 4⅞ in/124 mm
Specially Selected	Robustos	P	50 × 4⅞ in/124 mm
Gigantes	Prominentes	P	49 × 7⅝ in/194 mm
Small Club Coronas	Minutos	P	42 × 4⅜ in/110 mm

⊰ ROMEO y JULIETA ⊱

VITOLA DE SALIDA	VITOLA DE GALERA	FORMAT	SIZE
Belicosos	Campanas	F	52 × 5½ in/140 mm
Belvederes	Belvederes	P	39 × 4⅞ in/125 mm
Cazadores	Cazadores	P	43 × 6⅜ in/162 mm
Cedros De Luxe No.1	Cervantes	P	42 × 6½ in/165 mm
Cedros De Luxe No.2	Coronas	P	42 × 5⅝ in/142 mm
Cedros De Luxe No.3	Marevas	P	42 × 5⅛ in/129 mm
Churchills	Julieta No.2	P	47 × 7 in/178 mm
Churchills	Julieta No.2	P	47 × 7 in/178 mm
Churchills	Julieta No.2	P	47 × 7 in/178 mm
Churchills	Julieta No.2	P	47 × 7 in/178 mm
Club Kings	Marevas	P	42 × 5⅛ in/129 mm
Coronitas En Cedro	Petit Cetros	P	40 × 5⅛ in/129 mm

⊰ ROMEO y JULIETA ⊱

VITOLA DE SALIDA	VITOLA DE GALERA	FORMAT	SIZE
Exhibicion No.4	Hermosos No.4	P	48 × 5 in/127 mm
Julieta	Julieta No.6	P	33 × 4¾ in/120 mm
Mille Fleurs	Petit Coronas	P	42 × 5⅛ in/129 mm
Mille Fleurs	Petit Coronas	P	42 × 5⅛ in/129 mm
Petit Churchills	Petit Robustos	P	50 × 4 in/102 mm
Petit Churchills	Petit Robustos	P	50 × 4 in/102 mm
Petit Coronas	Marevas	P	42 × 5⅛ in/129 mm
Petit Coronas	Marevas	P	42 × 5⅛ in/129 mm
Petit Julietas	Entreactos	P	30 × 3⅞ in/100 mm
Petit Julietas	Entreactos	P	30 × 3⅞ in/100 mm
Regalias de Londres	Coronitas	P	40 × 4⅝ in/117 mm
Romeo No.1	Cremas	P	40 × 5½ in/140 mm
Romeo No.1	Cremas	P	40 × 5½ in/140 mm
Romeo No.1	Cremas	P	40 × 5½ in/140 mm
Romeo No.2	Petit Coronas	P	42 × 5⅛ in/129 mm
Romeo No.2	Petit Coronas	P	42 × 5⅛ in/129 mm
Romeo No.2	Petit Coronas	P	42 × 5⅛ in/129 mm
Romeo No.2	Petit Coronas	P	42 × 5⅛ in/129 mm
Romeo No.3	Coronitas	P	40 × 4⅝ in/117 mm
Romeo No.3	Coronitas	P	40 × 4⅝ in/117 mm
Romeo No.3	Coronitas	P	40 × 4⅝ in/117 mm
Short Churchills	Robustos	P	50 × 4⅞ in/124 mm
Short Churchills	Robustos	P	50 × 4⅞ in/124 mm
Short Churchills	Robustos	P	50 × 4⅞ in/124 mm
Sports Largos	Sports	P	35 × 4½ in/117 mm
Wide Churchills	Montesco	P	55 × 5⅛ in/130 mm
Wide Churchills	Montesco	P	55 × 5⅛ in/130 mm
Wide Churchills	Montesco	P	55 × 5⅛ in/130 mm

⊰ SAINT LUIS REY ⊱

VITOLA DE SALIDA	VITOLA DE GALERA	FORMAT	SIZE
Regios	Hermosos No.4	P	48 × 5 in/127 mm

⟨ *SANCHO PANZA* ⟩

VITOLA DE SALIDA	VITOLA DE GALERA	FORMAT	SIZE
Belicosos	Campanas	F	52 × 5½ in/140 mm
Non Plus	Marevas	P	42 × 5⅛ in/129 mm

⟨ *SAN CRISTOBAL de la HABANA* ⟩

VITOLA DE SALIDA	VITOLA DE GALERA	FORMAT	SIZE
El Principe	Minutos	P	42 × 4⅜ in/110 mm
La Fuerza	Gordito	P	50 × 5½ in/140 mm
La Punta	Campanas	F	52 × 5½ in/140 mm

⟨ *TRINIDAD* ⟩

VITOLA DE SALIDA	VITOLA DE GALERA	FORMAT	SIZE
Coloniales	Coloniales	Pt	44 × 5¼ in/132 mm
Coloniales	Coloniales	Pt	44 × 5¼ in/132 mm
Fundadores	Laguito Especial	Pt	40 × 7½ in/192 mm
Reyes	Reyes	Pt	40 × 4⅜ in/110 mm
Reyes	Reyes	Pt	40 × 4⅜ in/110 mm
Reyes	Reyes	Pt	40 × 4⅜ in/110 mm
Vigia	Torres	P	54 × 4⅜ in/110 mm
Vigia	Torres	P	54 × 4⅜ in/110 mm

⟨ *VEGAS ROBAINA* ⟩

VITOLA DE SALIDA	VITOLA DE GALERA	FORMAT	SIZE
Don Alejandro	Prominentes	P	49 × 7⅝ in/194 mm
Famosos	Hermosos No.4	P	48 × 5 in/127 mm
Unicos	Pirámides	F	52 × 6⅛ in/156 mm

⟨ *VEGUEROS* ⟩

VITOLA DE SALIDA	VITOLA DE GALERA	FORMAT	SIZE
Entretiempos	Petit Edmundo	P	52 × 4⅜ in/110 mm
Entretiempos	Petit Edmundo	P	52 × 4⅜ in/110 mm
Tapados	Mareva Gruesa	P	46 × 4¾ in/120 mm
Tapados	Mareva Gruesa	P	46 × 4¾ in/120 mm
Mañanitas	Mañanitas	F	46 × 3⅞ in/100 mm
Mañanitas	Mañanitas	F	46 × 3⅞ in/100 mm

INDEX

Page references in *italics* indicate photographs and illustrations
* indicates reference is to a footnote